C000272238

DANGEROUS WORK

DANGEROUS WORK

THE MEMOIR OF
PRIVATE
GEORGE WEEKS
OF THE
LABOUR CORPS
1917 – 1919

EDITED BY
ALAN WEEKS

Cover illustrations: *Front:* George in Cologne in 1919; Ypres mud,
1917. This is a road! (Australian War Memorial, negative E01318);
Back: Building a light railway. (IWM)

First published 2014
by Spellmount, an imprint of The History Press
The Mill, Brimscombe Port
Stroud, Gloucestershire, GL5 2QG
www.thehistorypress.co.uk

© Alan Weeks, 2014

The right of Alan Weeks to be identified as the Author
of this work has been asserted in accordance with the
Copyrights, Designs and Patents Act 1988.

All rights reserved. No part of this book may be reprinted
or reproduced or utilised in any form or by any electronic,
mechanical or other means, now known or hereafter invented,
including photocopying and recording, or in any information
storage or retrieval system, without the permission in writing
from the Publishers.

British Library Cataloguing in Publication Data.
A catalogue record for this book is available from the British Library.

isbn 978 0 7509 5667 3
Typesetting and origination by The History Press
Printed in Great Britain

CONTENTS

PREFACE

This is my father's account of his war experiences on the Western Front between 1917 and 1919, edited by me. This was handwritten after the war on seventy-eight sheets of cut-up wallpaper. They were in a box file left to me by my father. Notes and comments are included in the main text but are shown in a different font – this is to assist in the reading of the document, otherwise the reader would be continually looking up references elsewhere. I have added two simple maps so that the reader may follow George's movements in northern France and Flanders.

Alan Weeks

INTRODUCTION

In fifteen years of research into the role and activities of the Labour Corps this is the only soldier's diary I have ever seen. What makes it even more remarkable is the fact that for a corps that was to involve over 500,000 British officers and men there are only three known records and these were all by officers and written after the event when events could be judged in retrospect.

The diary makes interesting reading. It is the thoughts of a private soldier that have not been rewritten after the war. It does not involve great military actions but day-to-day survival in terrible conditions. It is quite obvious that world or national events have little or no concern to Private Weeks and his comrades who are involved in the daily grind of maintaining roads and railways.

The Labour Corps was one of a number of units that was formed during the war and disappeared soon after the war finished. Their activities are generally unsung and there were few formal records of their achievements; the units did not maintain war diaries. When Britain entered the European war in August 1914 all planning was based on a short war fought where local labour was easily available and tonnages of equipment were limited (siege warfare was not envisaged). France was different: most of the available manpower in France was conscripted to serve in the French Army and so the British Expeditionary Force (BEF) had to maintain its own supply lines.

When the BEF deployed it was mainly an infantry-heavy force with limited artillery and was not equipped for the drawn-out siege warfare experienced from November 1914 onwards. In 1914 the army was using about 10,000 tons of ammunition a month but by June 1917 this had risen to 230,000 tons a month. Add to this food, fuel (including fodder), trench stores (sandbags, props, pickets etc.), medical supplies and all the other equipment, and you can see what a massive effort was required to unload from ships in France, load trains, transfer to light railways and roads, and finally move stores to the front on mules and by men. It should be remembered these were the days before material-handling equipment and all stores were moved by hand. At the same time railways and roads were laid, upgraded and maintained by a significant uni-formed workforce.

The first labour units were deployed to France in early 1915 to work in the docks and maintain the railways. As the army grew, so did the demand for labour. In 1916, with the introduction of conscription, more men were being enlisted of lower medical category and over the accepted age limit of 35 for the infantry. These men, many suffering minor physical ailments like short-sightedness and from poor nutrition, were placed into infantry labour units and moved to France.

In April 1917 all the various forms of labour – infantry, Army Service Corps, Royal Engineers, prisoners of war etc. – were placed under a single command and the Labour Corps was formed. Many units did not take to being referred to as Labour Corps and you will note that George continually refers to the Queen's Regiment because his company, 132 Company Labour Corps, was previously 24 (Infantry) Labour Company the Queen's Regiment. Being a 'labourer' and not a 'soldier' had a certain stigma and as a result even the army ensured that medals and any graves were marked with the serviceman's original regiment (if he had one).

With the massive increase in labour units due to conscription there were still shortages. By November 1918 there were over 395,000 members of the Labour Corps. Eventually the British looked to their empire for support and Indians, Africans and West Indians came to France. By the end of the war there were 98,000 Chinese employed by the Labour Corps.

Following the war, the Corps was involved in battlefield salvage, which was to recover valuable material from the battlefield. It was not the British Army's problem to return the battlefield to farmland. Whilst carrying out this work the Corps also underook the task of concentrating the various battlefield graves into what are now the Commonwealth War Grave Commission cemeteries in France. This task proved so demanding that men who had left the service were asked to re-enlist to undertake burial duties.

George's diary makes interesting reading. He was a volunteer from a reserved occupation and being medically downgraded to C2 meant he did not have to join. His experiences reflect those of the many thousands of men who were in the Labour Corps; he has little knowledge of events outside his own section of twenty-eight men, and interestingly, even though he knows he joined 24 (Labour) Company, Queen's Regiment, when that forms into the Labour Corps he seems unsure of the company number. He reflects the attitude of many of the men transferred to the Labour Corps in that he continually refers to his 'old' regiment and cap-badge rather than the new organisation.

Throughout his service he visits all the main combat areas, starting with clearing up the old Somme battlefield, moving to Ypres to maintain roads during the battle of Passchendaele and, although not in the line during the March offensives, being actively employed in producing the GHQ Reserve Line. After the allied advance in August 1918 he followed the advancing army into German-occupied Belgium and finally into the occupied zone of Cologne.

His experiences show that although the Corps was not in the front line its members spent many long periods within the range of enemy artillery without relief. The front-line infantry tended to rotate between front line, support and reserve/rest/training (outside of enemy artillery range). George himself spends a long period at Kitchener Wood, Ypres, building an artillery-locating facility which is abandoned. Other records I have seen show men maintaining light railways, within the range of enemy guns for up to six months without a break. It must be remembered that all these men were of low medical category.

Although initially unarmed, the Labour Corps was not non-combatant. The non-combatant corps consisted of conscientious objectors, whereas the Labour Corps tended to be personnel who had been medically downgraded due to wounds or age. Had the original companies been armed, a lot of work would have been lost as the men undertook weapons training etc. Following the March 1918 offensive, a decision was made to arm the whole Labour Corps, to enable its men to defend themselves and certain areas of the line, but this took time.

George's Unit, 132 Company, although a labour company of five officers and 425 men, does not fully reflect all 300 British labour companies at the front. Since it was employed in relatively quiet zones it suffered remarkably few casualties, and there are only two recorded Meritorious Service Medals and no gallantry awards. Some units were unlucky and ended up bearing the brunt of the German advances in 1918.

I wish that this script had been available when I was researching the work of the Labour Corps as it fully represents the role played by many thousands of men, both British and foreign (Indians, Africans, Chinese etc.), within the corps in France.

Lt-Col. John Starling, (co-author with Ivor Lee of *No Labour, No Battle: Military Labour During the First World War*)

The Memoir of
Private
George Weeks

GEORGE IN NORTHERN FRANCE

ESTRÉE BLANCHE
30 MILES
NORTH WEST

ARRAS

• Barley

• Candas

• Mailly-Maillet

Beaumont-Hamel •

• Achiet-le-Grand

BAPAUME

• Courcelettes

Thiepval •

• Pozières

• Aveluy

• Contay

ALBERT

River Ancre

Canal du Nord

CAMBRAI

St Quentin Canal

ENGLEFONTAINE
FOREST OF MORMAL
20 MILES

1

MARCH 1917

At the beginning of March 1917, I was approaching my nineteenth birthday, which was the tenth of April. Little did I know that I was to celebrate this event on the Somme.

I was employed as a docker in the South West India docks, mostly discharging sugar from Cuba. This was extremely heavy labour: being tall, I was back-lifter in a piling squad consisting of five men. Although I was a near six-footer my weight was 9 stones, 2 lbs.

This waterway still exists some 200m south of Canary Wharf. The main (earlier) West India Dock waterways are also still there, about 200m north of Canary Wharf. The docks closed to commercial traffic in 1980.

I gradually realised I was being dehydrated through excess hard work and lack of nourishment. So the time had arrived when I decided to alter these circumstances.

On the first Monday of March a fresh consignment of sugar got through the submarine blockade. *[Unrestricted U-boat warfare resumed in 1917 with the German aim of forcing Britain to sue for peace. Outnumbered by 190 divisions to 150 on the Western Front, German hopes of victory there had dwindled. In this month 25 per cent of Britain-bound shipping was lost. The American president had severed all diplomatic relations with Germany (Congress declared war on 6 April). Germany hoped for a profitable peace settlement before the American Army was ready to fight in Europe.]*

The squad was busily engaged piling the heavy bags. After lunch, which was not a lot, I enraged the largest lout of the other four – at least twice my weight. He was under the mistaken impression that he could misname me with impunity. I answered this character so effectively that he attacked me, with the result that I received a cut and blackened eye.

I had noticed his bloated waistline swollen with the lunchtime imbibement of liquor, so after receiving a few blows he sank to the floor of the warehouse gasping like a great porpoise. I had landed the right blow in the right place.

Knowing full well that this incident would not end there (I was the outsider of the five) I decided to end my work there and burn my boats. I therefore proceeded to the Labour Office with the plea that medical attention was needed. My time and wages were made up and as I received my employment cards as well I had washed my hands of the docks for the time being.

Arriving home in Cubitt Town I bathed the eye, made tea and changed to outdoor attire, wearing one of my so-called two best suits, deciding to spend a couple of hours at the cinema.

Cubitt Town is the south-east part of the Isle of Dogs, East London, facing Greenwich across the Thames. William Cubitt, Lord Mayor of London 1860 to 1862, was responsible for the development of housing and amenities in this area in the 1840s and 1850s for workers in the local docks, shipbuilding yards and factories.

I took the bus to Poplar. At the Pavilion was showing 'The Battle of the Somme'.

The 'Pav', as we still called our favourite picture palace thirty years later, was situated at the junction of East India Dock and Cotton Street. The Battle of the Somme (1916) was one of the most successful British war films ever made. It is estimated that more than 20 million tickets were sold in this country in the first two months of its release. It was distributed worldwide in order to prove this country's commitment to the war. It is the source of many of the conflict's most iconic images. The film gave an unprecedented insight into the realities of trench warfare, controversially including the depiction of dead and wounded soldiers. It showed scenes of the build-up to the infantry offensive and the massive preliminary bombardment. Coverage of the first day of the battle – the bloodiest single day in the British Army's history – demonstrated the smallness of the territorial gains and the huge losses suffered to gain them. As a pioneering battlefield documentary, the very concept of The Battle of the Somme outraged commentators and set off a fierce debate about showing actual combat. The use of a staged sequence to represent the opening of the assault posed doubts about the documentary format.

It was horrifying to me, and at the back of my mind was the thought that I was classified C2, which meant passed for Home Service under the Lord Derby Scheme. [The 'Lord Derby Scheme' (officially the 'Group Scheme' – 'Group' referring to men's dates of birth and call-up dates) was abandoned at the end of 1915 because not enough potential recruits were coming through this voluntary (though morally persuasive) system. Real conscription arrived with the Military Service Act of January 1916. George must have been amongst the last men attested to under the Lord Derby Scheme because the last registrations for it were made in March 1916, when George was still 17 (he was born 10 April 1898).] I wouldn't be subjected to those terrible conditions.

C2 Medical Category meant 'C – temporarily unfit for service in categories A (fit for general service) or B (not fit for general service, but fit for service at home), but likely to become fit within six months, and for employment in depots; and '2' – able to walk to and from work a distance not exceeding 5 miles, see and hear sufficiently for ordinary purposes. The C2 medical classification was due to his chronic migraines. Moreover, the government had pledged not to send teenagers to the front line (by 1918 half the infantry was 19 or under!). Any pledge made by the Lord Derby Scheme not to send some men abroad was just as likely to fall foul of the pressing needs of the British Expeditionary Force. Of the men medically examined in 1917 and 1918 only 36 per cent were found fit enough for full military service; 40 per cent were physically unable to serve, even as non-combatants. Men of George's age were being called up by October 1916 but dockers were regarded as doing work of national importance.

On my way home the thought struck me that the way out for me was to join the Army. So next morning I travelled to the local recruiting office. After a great deal of discussion trying to persuade me to go to a munitions factory in the Midlands I was finally enrolled in a Works Battalion [it was a labour company of five officers and 425 men and not a labour/works battalion of thirty-six officers and 1,000 men] called the 24th Queen's Royal West Surreys, at that time stationed at the Rangers Drill Hall in Harrow Road, Paddington.

These men were also below the A1 medical grade required for full service but could be employed within the range of enemy artillery (again, George and his mates were certainly within range near Ypres in late 1917 and early 1918, and very definitely in extreme danger from enemy aircraft).

Arriving and reporting to this depot the next morning I realised that this was an entirely new unit formed with men from all over London with Categories B1 down to my low one. It took several days to start licking this outfit into shape. The drilling was no novelty to me. I had spent several years as a member of the Boy's Brigade and knew the basic drill prevailing at that period.

The catering arrangements were excellent. In sections we were taken to various coffee and dining rooms and supplied with substantial meals. I liked this. Around the third day we were taken by the lorry load to Park Royal Depot for kitting out. I was amazed at the efficient way this chore was accomplished. Some fellows were barely five feet tall, others six feet three inches plus. All were seen to at lightning speed.

About the fourth day since our enlistment the Unit came face to face with a fresh arrival – our Sergeant Major arrived from Hampshire, from the famous Green Howards. I have heard since that this Regiment is noted for quick step marching. [This is not the case for the Green Howards (Yorkshire Regiment) but would have been true for the Rifle Brigade (Green Jackets), and as the Rifle Brigade was a London-based unit it is more likely that this is where he was from.] No doubt he had been informed of the hard task awaiting him and was soon employed in turning us inside out. His favourite utterance was 'I'll liven you up, you people', and, funnily enough, he succeeded.

On the fifteenth of March, the Unit was inspected by the Commander of the whole London area – Major General Sir Francis Lloyd. He paused behind me and screwing his cane between my shoulder blades commanded me to 'Get that busby seen to', meaning that my hair needed barbering, of course.

Major-General Lloyd commanded the Brigade of Guards and was also General Officer Commanding London District. He was responsible for the defence of London, especially against Zeppelins. He had delegated powers over trains, hospitals, etc.

The Sergeant Major stated I was for the high jump and my name and number were taken down for some punishment to be doled out to me.

The next day, the sixteenth, a depressing rumour travelled around that the Battalion [company] was about to embark for France. There was not a lot of substance in this grapevine until mid-afternoon when dozens of Military Police arrived and all exits were sealed. The penny dropped. The next morning we were entrained for Folkestone and went aboard a famous Thames cruise vessel which was propelled by paddle wheels.

When the Unit arrived in early morning at Folkestone a ladle of vegetable soup was issued to each man. On the boat young lads were passing among us offering pork pies at two pence each. I purchased three of these. Afterwards I had good cause to reflect that stew and pork pie was not a suitable diet for a rather bumpy trip across the Channel.

The vessel arrived at Boulogne 17 Mar 1917. The crossing had been extremely rough and most of us were in a bad way. We still had to march through the town and up the hill to St Martin's Camp. Here we were shouted and screamed at by a bevy of Base Wallah NCOs, which did not improve our condition and demeanour very much.

Hardly had we settled in the bell tents allotted us when we were paraded again. The request was politely bawled out – 'All men able to play a musical instrument step two paces forward'.

Around twenty fellows did so. They were marched away, the rest of us dismissed. About a half hour later these unfortunates arrived back from their 'musical lesson' – emptying latrine buckets.

Happily, our stay in this hateful place was just the night. We were marched to a railhead the next morning, where we entrained, arriving at Aschew Woods in the early hours of the next morning. We had been allowed to remove our boots. Whilst we occupied these box trucks unfortunately the boots got mixed, with dire results. I was one of the unlucky ones with a size nine and one about size seven.

The next camp was some two miles from the railhead, and I, amongst a dozen others, had to march to this place wearing only one boot.

During the day, however, with a number of men missing from parade, the Section leaders received orders to adjust this matter, and the men wearing larger boots than their size foot were booked for fatigues at a later date.

After a day or so's rest in this delightful spot infested with rats the size of cats we moved to the delightful village called Mailly Maillet [to work on a railway crossing and in storage dumps]. My Section was extremely lucky: we were billeted in an hotel called the Hôtel-de-Ville. There was only one snag, only the cellar was left intact and that was the quarter allocated to us.

Our rations at this stage were reasonably adequate, much more than I was getting at home. A couple of days after our arrival the Unit was marched three miles or thereabouts across open country. The whole terrain was in a shocking mess. Shell craters, smashed houses and trees, graves, wire metal, all the carnage of modern warfare. It was the Somme battlefield, the one I was viewing at the cinema such a short time previously.

There is no doubt that George had arrived in a devastated area, but, in fact, this was the far northern sector of the battle zone, and it was in enemy hands throughout the Battle of the Somme. The area certainly suffered from British bombardment but the final environmental disaster was actually wreaked by the Germans themselves in 'Operation Alberich'. 'Operation Alberich' followed the decision of General von Ludendorff, the German Commander in the west, to substantially withdraw from the front line established between Vimy (British sector) and Chemin des Dames, near Soissons (French sector) to a newly constructed fortified defensive front called the 'Siegfried Stellung' (Hindenburg Line to the Tommies). These works had commenced in the autumn of 1916. The Hindenburg Line was composed of a series of gun emplacements arranged chequer-wise and backed by deep and strongly constructed dugouts scattered over a depth of up to 4 miles. The line stretched for about 70 miles. Ludendorff's thinking was that he would not be able to win a decisive battle on the Western Front in the current situation, therefore unbreakable defence was the answer, at least until Russia collapsed. It was possible that Britain would agree to a peace settlement in view of the submarine blockade of its coasts. Going back to the Stellung straightened out a potentially dangerous salient. Also the front would shrink by 25 miles and be held by thirteen or fourteen fewer divisions. So when George arrived the enemy front was now about 15 miles further to the east. At its broadest point, around St-Quentin, the Germans had withdrawn about 20 miles. German High Command ordered the destruction of everything in the withdrawal sector in order to make any Allied advance logistically difficult. Crossroads were mined and vast craters would force all wheeled traffic on to the sodden fields. Trees were felled across roads. It was a scene of unfettered destruction – orchards and crops went, and all livestock was driven away. Villages were knocked down, just leaving the red roofs on the ground along with the smashed furniture. Clever booby traps were littered about in everyday objects such as shovels and helmets. Wells were poisoned. This was all accomplished before George came on the scene – hence the wilderness he described, and hence the need for new communications across it. The Labour Corps was employed building road and light railways across the 'devastated area' in order to supply the new front line the other side of what had been no-man's land.

There were various other Units at this spot on our arrival, probably two or three thousand men. Among the chatter going on I detected the Canadian drawl.

As far as one could see stretched lines of white tape. On one side was a large dump of tools – pickaxes, spades, crowbars etc.

The order was given to the men to march by the dump of spades and each take one. Then we were told the project was a railway to be constructed towards Achiet-le-Grand.

This was a light (Decauville) narrow-gauge railway line along which trucks could be pushed by hand if required. It could be built far more quickly than a conventional line and reduced the need for local powered locomotion. The Decauville manufacturing company was founded by Paul Decauville, a French pioneer in industrial railways. His major innovation was the use of ready-made sections of track fastened to steel sleepers. It was easily transported. British, French and German engineers built thousands of miles of this track.

Our orders – no human or animal remains to be left between the tapes.

Some days the amount of bodies to be re-buried was so numerous that hardly any construction work was accomplished. It wasn't long before the line Regiments engaged on this work in between their spells in the trenches discovered that our Unit was an unarmed, non-combative one, and formed the impression, wrongly, that we were conscientious objectors. [Some concientious objectors, in the Non Combatant Corps (NCC) were also employed in France but mainly in quarries and in the forests – they were not employed directly on military work such as moving munitions etc. due to their religious/political beliefs.] One day this led to some trouble with a famous northern Regiment, one whose cap badge was an exploding bomb [probably the Northumberland Fusiliers].

This incident happened as follows: we were working in the vicinity of Star Wood. The northern Unit was allocated their tasks for the day.

The last man of their party was a huge fellow, in my opinion, a full heavyweight. The first man of our party was probably the smallest of our battalion. The whole morning, right up to the time we broke off for a mug of coffee and a small snack of bully beef or cheese, with a couple of 'No. Five' biscuits, this huge bully gave our man the maximum amount of abuse.

Bully beef (or corned beef) had been a staple food on British battlegrounds since the 1860s. Preserved meat was an official ration substitute for fresh meat. In the event, this substitution was very frequent because of the scarcity of fresh meat on and behind the front line. The only references to fresh meat in my father's account were the mutton chops provided at the Royal Flying Corps (RFC) base at Candas and the 'alleged' beef at Christmas 1917. Bully beef could be made more palatable by frying it with onions or crushed hard biscuits to make a hot hash. In whatever form it came the corn in the corned beef provided extra carbohydrates to fill up the soldiers' stomachs. Bully beef varied greatly in quality: Fray Bentos was considered the best. But when Edmund Blunden tried to feed a stray dog on W.H. Davies' bully beef it cleared off in disdain. The biscuits were usually taken with bully beef or cheese. George meant 'Number 5 biscuits'. These were generally supplied by Huntley & Palmer. Until 1917 the standard issue was Number 4. Perhaps Number 5 was better? They were as hard as dog biscuits and the soldiers often referred to them as 'those fucking biscuits' after episodes with their teeth. Indeed, in order to protect the molars they could be softened in water. They could certainly stiffen up any stew, being crammed with carbohydrates in order to assuage the pangs of hunger.

It so happened we also had a heavyweight – Big Joe, he was called and he arranged to change over places with tiny Kenny. Joe had had considerable ring experience in civil life. His main job was as a stevedore in the Royal Group of Docks. He belonged to one of our Champions Stables, namely 'Johnny Summers'.

No sooner had we all resumed our labours than this big fellow started a violent tirade against Joe, whose answers culminated in infuriating the northern man, to such an extent he rushed at Joe and attacked him.

In a few seconds he was flattened and took a very long count. When his comrades saw what had happened their actions and murmurs looked as if an ugly situation was developing, but happily the officers and NCOs arrived on the scene and probably nipped any conflict in the bud. After a conference with the officer in command our Unit was taken some hundred yards further towards Pozières and we resumed our labours in that locality.

Round about four o'clock that afternoon the skies lowered. It began to snow. As time went by one could say that a blizzard had developed. Our Commanding Officer [Captain L.D. Goldie] looked worried and finally gave the order to proceed back to the agreed point to entrain back to camp.

We did not know it but it transpired later that the train had already arrived. It picked up the northern troops and steamed back with them, thus leaving us abandoned around seven miles from our base.

Finally, our CO gave the order to start back along the line. By this time the snow was practically blinding us and it was rapidly getting dark. We had struggled back the four miles along the rail, but then the snow had blotted out the familiar landmarks from the line to the road leading to the village. It was sometime between seven and eight o'clock that I saw a light in the distance.

When I reached it, I found that it was Lieutenant Hammond [Lieutenant C.F.B. Hammond], who had been off-duty that day, holding a hurricane lamp. I explained the position to him and he packed me off to get my evening meal of stew, potatoes, rice and raisins, with tea and added rum. This was extremely welcome.

George had just returned from a 7-mile trek in a blizzard back to camp. Stew joined bully beef and hard biscuits as a basic diet for the soldiers – both in the front line and in the back areas – again packing their stomachs with carbohydrates in order to make them feel full up. The all-embracing hot stew was a great comfort, using any available leftovers. A popular saying on the Western Front in 1917 was 'if the sun rises in the east it is a sure sign that there will be stew for dinner'. I realise now why my father always cooked stew whenever my mother was away for a few days. He would set it up on the first day and let it simmer for days on end adding extra ingredients daily. By the last day it had a certain richness about it. Rice added even more body to any meal and raisins added a touch of sweetness. Tea had to be very hot, strong and heavily sweetened with sugar and condensed milk ('sergeant-major's tea' – in the sense that he would always get the best of anything) in order to sustain the soldier through the day and night, mug after mug of the hot, brown, nectar-like brew. Canteens were often rated according to the quality of their tea. My dad told me he had little difficulty in getting down ten pints in a day – no wonder the capacious German pickelhaube helmets were in great demand. Rum ('Tom Thumb') always lifted spirits. The warm glow of the strong, black elixir crept like fire down to the feet. Added to tea it gave the beverage extra restorative powers. Medical officers often related the length of their sick parade queues to the amount of rum doled out.

The letters 'SRD' were printed on every jar of rum (a 2-gallon grey and brown earthenware vessel popularly known as a 'grey hen'). It stood for 'Special Rations Department' but according to popular opinion it meant 'seldom reaches destination' or 'soon runs dry' or 'service rum diluted'. Such 'leaking' jars might be filled or topped up with water, nut oil, whale oil or even creosote.

I then set about making the billet as cosy as I could for the later arrivals, knowing full well the state of exhaustion they would be in. A lot of these poor fellows were old enough to have been my father. They came in eventually by ones and twos, some of them having to be thawed out.

Some were not found until the next day. One good point I remember very well was that a particularly good breakfast was issued. Afterwards, the youngest and nimblest were detailed to search for the missing rank and file. The CO had decided that he was not sending any parties to the Rail Construction Outfit that day.

We travelled in the direction of Beaumont Hamel. Here, we witnessed an extremely gruesome sight in a broken down traverse. Half-buried in the falling earth were the remains of a Scots and a German soldier. Both had rushed and bayoneted each other simultaneously.

We proceeded to Star Wood. Here we discovered the entrance to a large dugout, by its position a former German one. I, being the youngest, also the slimmest, was ordered to descend and look around. Armed with matches and a few candle ends I descended into the gloomy depths. A large number of the original steps had collapsed or had rotted. I reached the bottom of the shaft and lit the largest candle end.

I discovered it was quite large as dugouts go, containing about fifty 2-tier bunks. I went closer to these and I froze in my tracks. All were occupied by German dead. I lost no time in reaching the surface again and informed the officer of my discovery.

He then led us in the direction of the Serre Ridge and finally seemed satisfied that no one of our battalion was drifting around.

So back to Mailly Maillett. The aftermath of the long march back in the snow the previous evening was a sick parade of about fifty. There were some injuries, one man losing three fingers through an accident with a fuse.

2

APRIL 1917 – SOMME

By April 1 the railroad was rapidly approaching Achiet-le-Grand, its destination, when two platoons were moved to another area after kit inspections numbers three and four. Slightly over two hundred men boarded a fleet of lorries belonging to the Royal Flying Corps. We were taken to a small town called Candas. Here was situated No. 2 Depot of the Royal Flying Corps.

George was part of the detachment sent to help at the Royal Flying Corps No. 2 Depot at Candas. They would remain here until July.

We arrived very late and were billeted in local barns and other outbuildings. After a meagre meal we settled down to a night's sleep, which was interrupted about five o'clock in the morning with the entry of a party bringing our breakfast – mutton chops, potatoes, rice boiled with raisins, stacks of bread and butter and dixies of the best brew of tea we had seen since our arrival in France. It looked so good that everyone seemed afraid to touch the viands for some time, thinking that a mistake had occurred.

After this enjoyable repast the detachment mustered and marched to the main building of the Depot. All were detailed to various jobs under the supervision of Royal Flying Corps personnel.

I was allocated to a technical section under the control of Flight Sergeant O'Brien, handling all parts of aircraft, even to constructing the machines and preparing them for take-off on the runway.

A very interesting first day was spent by some of us. Around four in the afternoon our chaps were mustered and we marched about one mile from Candas to a disused camp, used to contain German prisoners, probably after the Somme battle.

Here we made ourselves very comfortable, and all seemed very happy. On the outskirts was a macadamised parade ground used by the Royal Flying Corps for licking into shape with pack drill those unfortunates who had bent the rules during the day.

We gradually got a bit edgy over the continuous barking and shouting of commands which rent the evening air, and so our fellows lined the fencing and did some shouting themselves. Gradually, the tyranny on the other side of the fence became more reasonable and let up a bit on the defaulters.

It was only a matter of time before some of this iron guard discipline rubbed off on us. Sergeant Tutt, a Boer War veteran, had been promoted Company Sergeant Major to our detachment. He was quite a genial person as a sergeant, but now the file soon started receiving some stick for trifling matters.

For instance, the matter of my long hair was recalled and as a reward I was sentenced to seven days' fatigues. I hadn't even known that a barber was available. After a hard day under F.S. O'Brien I paraded with around a dozen defaulters and was surprised to learn that we had a choice of two tasks, six men for cookhouse chores and the rest to bring some water from the village pump. I had visions of the black dixies in the cookhouse so voted for the water fatigue.

The conveyance was a huge wooden cask mounted on the front axle and wheels of a Crossley Tender, a very heavy-looking contraption. As we neared this object we discovered that the tyres were deflated. There was no way of remedying this so we took off to the village over one mile distant.

The RFC made much use of Crossleys. The heavy chassis could carry ambulances, mobile workshops or light trucks. Each RFC squadron was supposed to have nine Crossleys but they often had less than this. Elderly ones could obviously be adapted for other uses.

At the well the water had to be hauled up to the surface, then transferred to the interior of the cask by bucket. The bung hole was about 3 inches in diameter so consequently a good half of the liquid was spilled. When the cask was full a back-breaking trip confronted us. The way back to camp was a gentle rise all the way.

On our arrival the information was given to us that this load was to be emptied into a tank adjoining the cookhouse and that a second one was required for officers and ablutions use. The language on the second trip in both ways was indescribable. Finally, this matter became so rough on the troops that other ideas had to be used – the sensible one having the water obtained by a daily fatigue party, a trapdoor cut into the top of the cask and, most importantly, towed mechanically to the camp.

After a few days of water fatigues I had a day's excuse. We were accorded the privilege once a month. As soon as possible, I made a bee-line to the barber's tent. He sat me on a box, draped a clinging towel round my neck and enquired how I wanted the hair trimmed. He listened carefully, and then proceeded to run the clippers from my forehead clean to the nape of my neck. I remarked that scissors would not be necessary and in a few minutes I was ready to leave, with only my ears saving my cap from blindfolding me. Thus, I became the main source of merriment for everyone around but it wasn't long before number twos became fashionable for everyone. Anyway, it was sensible and hygienic.

The following Monday (April 9) was a bustling day. Some huge cases had arrived and our first job was to transfer these to the air strip, which was a large meadow kept closely mowed. We ascertained that a fighter machine was to be assembled, one that had not been seen before, a new product of the Royal Aircraft Factory, named the S.E. 5.

It turned out to be a super plane but only a minority of squadrons were supplied with them. The SE5s, along with the far more plentiful Sopwith Camels, enabled the RFC to recover from the severe losses of 'Bloody April' and assume superiority in the air for the rest of the war. The SE5 came from the Royal Aircraft Factory at Farnborough. Some 5,205 were built.

All the squad kept hard at this task all day till dusk, hardly stopping to eat. Our work was covered for the night. We resumed next morning to complete the machine. I was helping to install the motor and noticed the name of the manufacturer. This seemed to be foreign. I thought it sounded Spanish to me. Another innovation was the machine gun facing directly forward in front of the pilot seat.

Our remarks about the effect of a rain of bullets on the propeller generally amused Flight Sergeant O'Brien, who proceeded to give us a brief lecture on synchronisation, proving to our satisfaction that the bullets would by-pass the propeller when its position was north and south and not east and west, a complete explanation to our simple minds.

Sometime around noon a Crossley Tender arrived with two occupants, one a flying officer. I noticed that he wore three stars on his shoulder straps: he was a

Captain. A rumour travelled around that this was a well-known Ace and that he was taking this machine on trials and tests.

Sometime later the machine was declared ready. The pilot donned a Sidcot suit and took charge of the controls and started to familiarise himself with them. [Sidney Cotton was an Australian inventor and photographic expert. He was most influential in the development of reconnaissance photography during the war. He was also a combat pilot and designed the 'Sidcot', a flying suit which kept pilots warm in the air. It was used by the RFC and later the RAF until the 1950s. Unfortunately, he fell out with senior RFC officers and resigned his commission in October 1917.] Within the hour he flew away and became just a dot on the skyline. Even today, when I ponder over the past years, the thought crossed my mind – was this the great and tragic Captain Ball?

It was! Captain Albert Ball had just returned from a spell of service in England to become a flight commander with the elite No 56 Squadron at Vert Galant base (7 April). The packing case George helped with contained Ball's new SE5 – number A4850. Ball had actually arranged for the removal of the synchronised Vickers machine gun, to be replaced with a second Lewis gun fitted to fire downwards through the floor of the cockpit. Also a red propeller boss from a German LVG he had previously shot down was fitted to his plane. But when my father saw him on Monday, 9 April the synchronised gun had been reinstated, which is why Flight Sergeant O'Brien was able to explain about it. The photograph on page 73 shows Captain Ball in A4850 – this is how George saw him. As a matter of fact, Albert Ball was not at all happy with the SE5 and was allowed to keep his Nieuport 17 for his solo missions. He only flew the SE 5 on patrol with the rest of the squadron.

Summer was rapidly approaching and the sky war was intensifying after the battle of Vimy Ridge. All kinds of aircraft were making emergency landings on the airfield. Sometimes the pilots were in a bad shape, some even dead when taken from the cockpit. One of my tasks was to patch up bullet holes with the quick-drying dope and treated linen squares and circles provided for this purpose.

The battle at Vimy Ridge began on the day George saw Captain Ball – 9 April. The newly arrived Canadian Corps secured a famous victory up this slope which had held back the Allies for three years. Little further advance in Artois was achieved, however, against the new powerful, flexible Stellung defences. The campaign had stalled by the time the French launched their offensive at the Chemin des Dames (16 April). In the air the RFC suffered 'Bloody April' – seventy-five planes and nineteen pilots lost between 4 and 9 April when the British fighters were trying to clear the way for proper reconnaissance of enemy positions. The French (Nivelle) attack bogged down just as rapidly as the British offensive. It suffered ever-increasing losses – 100,000 men by 9 May. This led to growing mutiny in the ranks and the new commander, Pétain, had to make big changes in order to appease the disgruntled soldiers. As a result the French could contemplate no further major offensives for a considerable time. It was the BEF who would have to take the initiative – to the north, in Flanders.

3

MAY 1917

Early in May I was one of fifty men detailed for a new project. The need had arisen for dozens of new airfields and accommodation for the attending staff required for the maintenance of same. We were known as the 14th T.D. Party. In charge of this Unit was an officer we had left behind in Mailly Maillett, Lieutenant R. Cousins, who was a contractor in civil life. We were unaware of it at the time, but it was stated later that he undertook to construct and complete an airfield in fourteen days.

The first one took ten days. This was adjacent to a village on the Belgian border named Estrée Blanche. Our C.O. was a worker himself and joined in every project.

The hangars of those days were of heavy canvas stretched over timber framing. The accommodation was called Nissen Huts. All the paths around the airfield were constructed of shale, the waste product of the local coalmines.

George was at the airfield at Estrée-Blanche. Nissen huts were designed by Major Peter Nissen of the Royal Engineers. Between August 1916 and the end of the war around 100,000 were manufactured. These structures were economical with materials (semi-cylindrical elephant-iron sheets), could be transported and stored easily (the sheets could be cupped inside each other) and could be erected by six men in four hours – but one was put up in eighty-seven minutes! They were usually 30ft in length. Number 56 Squadron had moved to the first one built by the Queen's at Estrée-Blanche in May.

The Lieutenant was a complete driver. We rose at 5 o'clock in the morning and worked extremely hard – till around 6 in the evening. But he had no interest in spit and polish. He was very hard on the cooks. He made sure that we worked on full stomachs.

4

JUNE–AUGUST 1917 – SOMME

One very sultry night we lay on the floors of the Nissen Huts finding difficulty in dropping off to sleep. Around midnight or later a great blaze of light appeared in the sky, and then came the heaviest explosion I have ever experienced. The nearest approach to this eruption before this was the one from the Brunner Mond chemical factory which devastated Silvertown in East London. We had one man hurt: his steel helmet was hung on a rail above his head. He received a severe cut and we lost his services for a few days. Information later received was that Hill 60 had been mined (June 7).

This explosion was actually at 3.10 a.m. below Messines Ridge. Nineteen enormous mines were detonated. A geology professor in Lille was convinced it was a proper earthquake: it was also detected on a seismograph on the Isle of Wight. The war correspondent, Philip Gibbs, wrote: 'there gushed out and up enormous volumes of scarlet flames ... earth and smoke all lifted up by the flames spilling into mountains of fierce colour, so that the countryside was illuminated by red light.'

The Hill 60 explosion was the first move by the British after the French failure in the south. The advent of the Americans was a long way off and with the prospect of hundreds of thousands of German troops transferring from the Eastern Front something had to be done to keep the enemy in check. The attack at Messines was a curtain-raiser, the aim of which was to gain the southern heights of a long ridge running into Belgium to the north-east of Ypres. The Germans held a formidable hold on this ridge. But even with this massive blow at Messines (of about a million tons of TNT) only a limited advance was made against the in-depth and flexible enemy defences. All depended on the major offensive east out of Ypres towards Passchendaele on the ridge just 6 miles away.

The eruption from the Brunner Mond chemical factory which devastated Silvertown in East London occurred on 19 January 1917. It was the biggest East London explosion ever. The factory was flat out producing shells when it went up. It was situated amongst hundreds of houses which were destroyed. Seventy-three residents lost their lives and hundreds were badly injured. The chemical factory was lying idle at the start of the war and was converted to war production due to the serious shell shortage in 1915. Placing a TNT factory in such a crowded area was a huge risk.

After a few weeks of this construction activity we proceeded back to Candas and carried on with our former duties, till later in June we were re-called to our main Unit in Mailly Maillet. A few days later we were paraded in full kit and then started a very long march to another village on the Somme. This was called Contay – in a good farming area and with no apparent destruction from enemy action. [This move was in July 1917 and the work continued until September 1917.]

High above the village rose a great hill surrounded by dense woods. This was our next objective – demolishing the trees for timber urgently needed in the front lines. We had to have expert tuition once again, and like our railroad building experience we were overseen by probably the greatest timber-felling experts ever known – the Canadian Forestry Corps.

The corps was founded in November 1916 to manage the assembly of the huge quantities of timber needed in the front lines – duckboards for trench floors, shoring planks and crates etc. The initial idea was to get the wood from Canada and ship it over but space was at a premium in the merchant ships so it was decided to get supplies from the UK and France. By the time of the Contay project there were over 30,000 Canadians in the Corps. They also assisted in the construction of RFC airfields, piling up artillery shells and building roads and railways.

The work started in great fashion. We were divided into sections of forest and required to produce a certain amount each day. I was in the fascines group. The surplus cuttings from the trees and undergrowth enabled our allotted contribution of fascines to be completed in less than five hours. But as the material grew scarcer so did our time in these woodlands become longer – nine hours, then ten, twelve and so on. From the higher-ups no allowance had been made for this fact.

5

SEPTEMBER 1917– SOMME AREA

The Unit was kept at this task till early September, when the supply of raw material had completely dwindled. A few days was spent on drilling and patching up the local roads. These latter were always in need of repair so the nearest troops automatically fell in for this work.

A new venture was brought about by one of the officers. He proposed forming a football team after discovering that there happened to be at least eight professional footballers among our ranks. One difficulty he experienced was finding a goalkeeper. He surmounted this obstacle by appearing in the billets after evening meal, accompanied by the Orderly Sergeant.

Naturally, everyone present sprang to attention immediately. He eyed me and asked my name. He turned to the Orderly Sergeant, nodded, and my name was added to others in the book he was carrying. So I had volunteered as the new goalkeeper.

For the following few weeks, instead of seven or eight hours work on road-mending, I, among the others elected for the team, went on training runs and were taken to distant bathing establishments and managed to get to a YMCA canteen, where we were able to stock up on goodies.

We also took part in about three so-called friendly games a week. We all collected the cuts and bruises to endorse how friendly these games were.

During this relaxing period a Colonial outfit arrived and were quartered in the village. This caused immediate inflation as the pay these fellows received topped ours enormously. Prior to their arrival we were able to obtain very easily eggs, milk, salads and bread at a very cheap rate. The advent of their Unit put these desirables out of our financial reach and a certain amount of resentment resulted.

One day open conflict flared up. We had two boxers, one I have already mentioned, Joe the heavyweight, and also a well-known featherweight who hailed from Custom House in Dockland. In some way they were able to skip various parades and duties, always seemed to have well-lined pockets, so were able to spend time and money in one of the local estaminets, where they practically lived in one of the small cubby holes or bars.

An estaminet was usually a small café. If the residents of a house or cottage were feeding and watering themselves, then why not extend this to paying customers? In November 1917 the small village of Marœuil had sixty-five such establishments. They made tea or coffee and sold surplus wine or very weak and sometimes watered-down beer – home-made or bought in from relatives or friends. Above all, the soldiers craved for egg and chips, and this was no problem in a French village. There were some large establishments, probably predating the war and employing a small staff of cooks and waiters, very often of the young and female variety in order to drum up custom. But most estaminets were modest places where the British soldier could sit on a chair or a bench, eat at a table in a warm room and clink glasses of 'plonk' ('van blong') with a pal, muttering 'bon chance' and the like. They called them 'just-a-minutes', which gives you some idea of their priority in the soldier's highly limited free time. There is a lot more detail on estaminets in my book Tea, Rum and Fags: Sustaining Tommy.

One day four Colonials entered this little compartment which was occupied by Joe and Steve. Whether by accident or otherwise their beer was knocked over on the table and a strong request for replacing the same was refused with some accompanying derision.

The result of this disagreement – four men badly knocked about plus damage to the inn, tables and chairs and a door, and arrests made by the Military Police. Joe and Steve received some stick from our C.O., mainly for not being where they were supposed to be that day, and the local estaminets were declared out of bounds to all troops.

GEORGE IN FLANDERS

FRANCE

BELGIUM

ST. OMER

HAZEBROUCK

St. Sylvestre Cappel

Forest of Nieppe

BOULOGNE
30 MILES

Poperinge

ARMENTIÈRES

YPRES

Flamertinge

Brielen

Elverdinge

Yser Canal

Hellfire
Corner

St-Jean

St-Julian

Kitchener's Wood

Langemark

Passchendaele

Roulers

Menin

Menin Road

6

OCTOBER 1917 – YPRES SALIENT

Early in October, with little or no work available locally, kit inspections were ordered, and it was rumoured that we would be moving on shortly. Finally, we undertook a long march to a railhead and entrained once again in the sumptuous box trucks, which was the usual mode of transport for long distances (October 10).

The Unit moved from the Somme area to Poperinghe in the Ypres Salient. Most of the work would be road and rail maintenance.

At the first stop made to relieve our cramped limbs and for other purposes, a whisper by someone who was never discovered suggested that the Unit was travelling northwards to England. This caused great excitement among the majority of the men. I hardly thought this could happen.

It was quite apparent that everyone was fitter and healthier since we had arrived in France and that there was no point in taking the Unit to the homeland. I rather suspected that other things were in store for us, and a few hours later my suspicions were confirmed.

By the end of the war George had increased his early 1917 body weight by 40 per cent. Men of the 7th Battalion of the Royal Sussex Regiment were actually measured: their average development in six months was an extra inch in height and a stone in weight. It was all those carbohydrates: Alfred Burrage described his comrades as 'perambulating stomachs'.

Generally the good diet and physical work did improve many of the men of the Labour Corps. Every month soldiers within the Corps were medically examined to see if they were fit to be transferred back to fighting units.

We knew we had steamed into Paris, and after a brief stay steamed eastwards. The rumbling which had assailed our ears got louder. We finally stopped at a very large railway centre and were ordered to make ourselves comfortable till daylight, which we proceeded to do, still worried somewhat about the noise which assailed our ears. One hour or two later we were ordered out and formed into respective platoons ready to march away to our destination.

Just then some lorries arrived which were to transport the stores and equipment. I was one of a party detailed to assist in loading these vehicles. I asked one driver what the district was, where we were bound and what the noise was. His reply was that where we were standing was a place called Poperinge, the stores, baggage and equipment were destined for a rest camp called Elverdinge, the noise was made by the guns round Ypres and the adjoining salient.

Poperinge was a critical hub in the supply to the Ypres Salient, about 10 miles from Ypres. The main attack, of what was to become known as 3rd Ypres, against the Gheluvelt plateau had begun on the last day of July. But the strong German defences had made progress impossible, along with the rain – five times as heavy as in 1915 and 1916. This and the massive British bombardments wrecked the drainage systems between Ypres and Passchendaele, turning the area into a sea of mud. General Plumer took over from General Gough on 20 September with some new ideas, but also not good enough to defeat the Germans or the mud. Field Marshal Haig was advised on many occasions to give up but he still had in mind the overall objective of preventing any major enemy offensive. The huge losses suffered by the defenders (possibly 250,000 – similar to British casualties) were instrumental in achieving this, at least until the spring of 1918. By the time George arrived at Poperinge the prospect of victory at Ypres had all but faded away, but all he and his comrades knew was that a savage battle was in progress on the other side of the Yser Canal, and that their lives were in peril.

In the meantime the Company had moved on, and some time later, on completing the loading the lorries took off in the same direction and to hasten us on our way a huge shrapnel shell burst high overhead, our driver remarking that this was the type the enemy fired at observation balloons.

The balloons were tethered to steel cables and winched up to about 3,000ft and winched down again when the required information had been collected. By 1917 they were greatly improved compared to those used at the start of the war – easier to fly and more resistant to bad weather, and kite-shaped to point into the wind. Balloons were defended in the same way as they were threatened – by guns and planes. Indeed, attacking a balloon could be a very dangerous assignment. There were some famous 'balloon-busters', such as the American pilot Frank Luke.

We proceeded several miles along the road and were greeted with another heavy explosion. This one was on the ground and as other traffic slowed up in front we were compelled to do likewise. Then a large crowd of blue-clad Orientals came rushing past us. They looked Chinese to me. They were obviously extremely frightened.

The British and French governments had signed an agreement to bring 80,000 Chinese labourers to the Western Front – a Chinese Labour Corps. They started arriving in France in April 1917. By the autumn of 1918 there were 98,000 of them in France and Belgium. The British Army provided officers and NCOs and the Chinese provided gangers. The terms of service were complex but generally they were not to be employed within the range of enemy artillery, although many were bombed from the air. They had Chinese students with them as translators but it didn't take them long to pick up some pidgin English (and French). A Fusilier tried to flog a duff watch to one of them but got the retort 'No bloody bonny-la!'

Everything started to move on again and as we passed a water-filling station we could see what had occurred. A G.S. wagon had received a direct hit. The horses were on one side of the road, badly mutilated and the unfortunate driver's remains were being placed on a stretcher, starting with a pair of legs.

This was a Mark X 'General Service' horse-drawn wagon, able to go where motorised vehicles could not (especially in the Flanders mud). They could carry food, fodder, barbed wire, ammunition – anything. It was a very tough vehicle, able to withstand all types of weather and road conditions.

Some time later the rest camp was reached. Our party unloaded the lorries and awaited the arrival of the main group. We were very subdued and hungry. Eventually the Company arrived and the cooks got busy preparing a meal, which was later very much appreciated.

Some days later we were moved on once more to another camp at Flamertinge. This consisted of Nissen Huts fortified half way up the walls with sandbags.

Running along the front of the camp was a railway apparently used to bring sand for various uses. But apparently there was one use we were to be made aware of the same evening which brought more shocks to our nervous systems.

It was dark when the bugler called for the evening meal to be collected. I was one of the last to collect the stew, potatoes, rice and tea and as I approached the hut an apparently loaded train arrived and stopped level with the huts. I entered the hut and placed my food on to the floor in order to take my knife, fork and spoon from my haversack.

My neighbour asked me about the arrival outside. I answered that I thought it was a new consignment of sand, and, according to the shouts and commands rending the air, the unloading was going to take place at express speed.

A second or two later there was a blinding flash followed by a terrific report. My supper rose several feet in the air and cascaded to the floor. We all rushed to the doorway to find that a massive gun mounted on railway bogies had just been fired.

Mounted on the train was a very large gun which was about to perform. Many of these howitzers were ex-naval pieces (known as 'Langer Max' by the Germans). The wagons on which they travelled had to be specially modified. The main problems for a railway gun were how to traverse the barrel to aim at its target, since the railway was usually in a fixed direction, and horizontal and vertical recoil. For traversing, a curved track or a turntable could be employed, or the transporter could be moveable on its mounts, or the gun could move within the truck. My father often described the incident to me and from what he said I gather that the gun appeared to move within the transporter. It used a 12-inch shell (the same as the fixed howitzer he later witnessed at the Ypres waterworks). The biggest shell was used in the German 'Big Berthas' – 16.5 inches.

At fairly quick intervals five more shells were fired and then the contraption was steaming back in the direction from which it had come. There was left a mess for me to clear up and I dined off a couple of hard tack biscuits. We were all wondering about what would happen next when three whistle blasts indicated that enemy aircraft were about, and all ranks were ordered to leave the huts and scatter into the open spaces around.

As we gazed upwards a large greeny-bluish light began to slowly descend from the night sky above, practically pinpointing the place where the gun had been fired from. Then one saw the lighted fuses of falling bombs. Happily for us, they fell two or three hundred yards away, but unfortunately on to some horse lines, destroying a score or more of the innocent animals.

An uneasy night followed. We all wanted to be away from the camp knowing how near the German bombs had exploded the previous evening. After an early breakfast fatigue parties were employed on interring the poor dead horses. This was always a depressing business to be involved in.

During the morning it seems our C.O. had not minced his words in condemnation of the risks we had all endured the previous evening, and by noon we were mustered and marched away. We came to a large open space near a chateau. This field had a narrow brook running around three sides. Among the stores accompanying us were forty or so bell tents, suitably camouflaged, which we began to erect. The method used in erecting the tents was as follows: a line of 3-inch circular stakes at even distances apart were driven into the ground, leaving about two feet above the surface. Then the tent was erected from the top of the stake, with the roof guys fully tautened. Then the trailing walls were tied up to the roof and the intending fifteen or sixteen prospective occupants got to work digging the interior earth, which was transferred to sandbags. A circular wall was built around the tent. The bags were lashed into position and shape by spades wielded by the men. Then more soil was thrown in a sloping gradient the height of the sandbags. When this operation was completed the wall of the tents was untied and lowered then secured to the base pegs.

This was the only time we had spent under canvas since our first arrival in France at St Martin's Camp, Boulogne the previous March.

There was nothing specially provided for the officers. They were also accommodated in bell tents, the only difference being they had more space to move around in.

Later, the lorries arrived bringing sectioned sheeting for ablutions, cooking and storage needs. We were kept hard at work till dusk erecting these. The cooks were not idle and prepared a substantial supper for everyone – bully beef and bean stew, potatoes boiled in their jackets, rice and raisins for seconds and an approximate pint of tea laced with rum.

And so to bed, everyone wondering what the morning held in store. The next day found the entire company except the permanent camp staff marching on the road towards the Yser canal bridge (October 18). Crossing this well-known structure we deployed to the right and met some Royal Engineer personnel. We collected spades and discovered that the project was that a two-inch cable was to be buried some six feet below the surface parallel to the canal bank.

The deep burying of cables provided protection against artillery fire, but should they be damaged, finding the break and subsequent repair was a major task. Surface laying was much easier but the ground tended to become a network of damaged unused cables. Labour Corps and Infantry units spent many hours burying telephone cables.

We all dug industriously but were annoyed at the conditions, having to be constantly pulled from the porridge-like mud, sometimes sinking almost to the waist. One man wearing waders accidently lost one, which had to stay in the mud. He was rescued as we broke off for midday refreshment, this usually being a couple of biscuits known as 'No. Fives' and a small piece of cheese or a slice of bully beef, known universally as corned beef.

We were greeted by a thunderous crack high overhead. I recognized the colour of the light brown smoke following the flash of the bursting shell as similar to the one I had seen explode over Poperinge railhead on our initial arrival.

After labouring several days on this project I realised that I was developing trouble with my feet. I had accidentally left my spare pair of socks behind at Contay, drying on a makeshift line. One thing that I discovered was that Army boots were excellent provided one wore two pairs of woollen socks. This prevented slipping and friction.

When I arose this particular morning I could not put my boots on because of the pain, swelling and a dozen or more nasty-looking sores around the heels.

One good pal brought my breakfast, and I was reported sick by the NCO acting as orderly. Later the medical orderly inspected my feet and listed me to visit the doctor, and, as I proved to his satisfaction that it was impossible to don my boots he obtained a very large pair of slippers for me to wear.

I was conveyed to the surgery, which I think was situated at Elverdinge. On entering the reception room I noticed three Orientals sitting on a bench looking very sorry for themselves. They may have belonged to the group I had last seen rushing along the Poperinge road. These men went first to the doctor's little cubby hole. As only a blanket separated it from the reception room I could not help but overhear the conversation that ensued. Apparently, they were suffering from some stomach complaint, but they received no sympathy from the 'kindly' doctor, who ordered the medical orderly to give them three 'No. Nines' each and a shovel to dig themselves in.

The British Army Number Nine pill was a laxative, so hopefully the labourers were suffering from constipation (a common complaint in the war zone) rather than the opposite. The No 9 was the classic treatment for men put on M and D (medicine and duty) or NYD (not yet diagnosed).

The No. 9 was also known as the 'Star of the Movies' and used in the soldiers' games of bingo – 'doctor's orders, number nine'.

I was then summoned to his august presence. His first question to me was why wasn't I in an infantry regiment. I pointed out that I had left England medically adjudged Category C2.

He then ordered me to strip and subjected me to a thorough medical examination. It seemed a long while before he was convinced my Category was genuine, and then proceeded to look at my, by then, very painful feet. His final diagnosis was treatment and duty. His orderly supplied me with lint boracic and other remedies, and I was taken back to camp.

A little while later the Sergeant Major (he was a new one, by the way – joining our outfit a little while previous to our departure from the Contay woodlands) came to the tent. He was a good sort and realised my plight in only being able to wear slippers on my feet and said I was to stay put in the tent. He would call me when I was needed – which was very nice treatment.

All the remainder of that day I was able to rest and keep the weight off my feet, somebody even bringing my lunch, saving me trudging through the thick mud to the cookhouse. This easy time lasted for three days, then the medical Corporal appeared bringing an extremely large size of cut-down Wellingtons which I was able to don with extra dressing and two pairs of Neurosocks.

He conveyed the Sergeant Major's instructions that I was to make myself useful round the camp, starting with the ration cart when it arrived – mucking in to unload it, helping the cooks.

Beside the food stores was a fairly large tank, two large cans made into makeshift pails and a milkmaid's yoke. This latter object completely puzzled me. What is it for? I asked myself.

Later that day Philip, the camp policeman, who was also my special pal, came to me and said that I was to assist him in a small task; the tank was to be installed adjacent to the officers' quarters. Apparently the Belgian brook water was upsetting their palates, and the tank was the answer. Fresh water was to be brought from the pump at Flamertinge alongside the railway line, and whoever was on fatigues would be bringing it by means of the pails and milkmaid's yoke.

I didn't have to be told – knowing full well that I was the most likely candidate for this operation. Sure enough, our kindly Sergeant Major appeared and asked me to try the job. So away I started along the railway lines for the water.

My feet stood up fairly well, the track was fairly smooth and my feet were fairly well padded. I found that I could fill the tank in roughly three hours. I also found a good hideout for the two cans, which I hid away full of water with the object of appearing with them simultaneously as the ration cart arrived so that I might possibly get out of assisting with the unloading.

The following day (October 27) this subterfuge was successful and as my feet were fairly comfortable I began exploring the surroundings, such as dugouts and other interesting structures. One dugout was evidently formerly an artillery abode. At the entrance was a boot scraper composed of corn beef tins. Idly digging at this I found that the tins were full. Inside the dugout I found a convenient sandbag and soon the tins of meat were on the way to the tent.

I then made my way to the cookhouse, enquiring if they needed assistance. Receiving a negative answer I managed to scrounge some vegetables. At the tent a petrol can with a top corner cut away in the form of a triangle was available and soon nearly two gallons of stew were bubbling away on our home-made stove – very highly appreciated by my comrades when they arrived back from the other side of the canal bridge.

Next day I carried on with the water fatigue without waiting for instructions. No one seemed to realise that I had dodged the unloading of the rations. On my third journey to the water tower I had just passed the horse lines when there was an eruption behind me, and all went blank and black.

I came to with several soldiers bending over me. Right close to me was a large segment of animal, which looked like part of a horse. I was smothered with earth and blood splashes from the horse's remains. One of the men found my helmet, which had received a broken strap.

In a little while I was able to get to my feet. I found that I was a little dizzy, and after a little further resting was able to take the cans, which I found undamaged, to get them refilled, after which I carried them back to the tank.

I then made my way to see Philip in his own private dugout which he was allowed to occupy owing to the unusual hours of his duties.

After explaining what had happened he turned to and started to clean me up, providing me with a cup of char (better known as tea). He enquired whose blood was on my uniform. It belonged to a horse was my reply.

I stayed and rested as long as possible. Philip was such a valuable friend. Later, in civilian life, we met up again. He took a position with a Millwall timber firm, quite close to where I lived. He passed away in his thirty fourth year, through chest cancer.

When I left the police dugout I felt more composed and refreshed. My tunic was still marked with the blood from the horse, but not a lot to take notice of.

I had made one resolve in the back of my mind – by hook or by crook I was going to get out of the officers' water-carrying chore by any means possible.

Whilst I was musing over this point the flap of four tent was opened and the head of the Sergeant Major appeared in the aperture. 'What's happened to you, Weeks?' he questioned. I told what had occurred. He then examined my helmet and said that I would have to have the chin strap replaced, and that I was excused duty for a few days. He would order a replacement for the water fatigue.

This suited my mood very well. As he left the tent, I decided if possible I would extend the excused duty for a week or more. My tent mates arrived later. They appeared downcast at first (there was nothing cooking and no hot water for shaving) but showed concern when they learnt what had happened to me.

I spent the next day very quietly. I managed to participate in a little dugout-scrounging, even obtaining some sandbags full of coal, and spent most of the afternoon with my pal in his shelter.

When my tent mates arrived back they were delighted the tent was clean and tidy and with a gallon and a half of bully stew, and also shaving water on top of a glowing coal fire awaiting them.

The next day was a repeat performance but on the third I was hardly able to obtain any tinned rations from the obsolete dugouts. There was only the fire and the shaving water for the men when they trudged back from their duties. I overheard a few muttered grumbles and I realised that extras I was providing were being taken as a matter of course, and decided that my only remedy would be to parade with the working parties once again.

7

NOVEMBER 1917 – YPRES SALIENT

N ext morning I could not arise at all – an attack of migraine was with me. It was one of my family legacies. My only relief in a bad attack was to keep in bed and cover my head to exclude all light.

During the day the medical Corporal called and insisted that I visited the doctor the next morning. I was not too happy about this but the pain I was experiencing at the time forced me to agree.

By the morning the migraine had disappeared and I joined the sick parade. I was surprised by the medical reception after I explained what had happened to me. He ordered 'Shirt off!' and started examining me closely.

'What's this blood on your neck?' he asked. I told him about the horse. He looked closer.

'It's not,' he exclaimed. 'You collected a wound at the back of your head. You've had a bad shake-up,' he said. 'If you had reported sick the day after this happened I would have sent you home. In the meantime take seven days excused duty.'

I came away thinking how unlucky can one get. There was nothing much to do during the next few days. I continued my exploration of dugouts and was fortunate in finding some clothing – underclothing and, particularly useful, a tunic.

I busied myself cleaning these articles. These finds enabled me to discard the stained tunic, dispensing with the need of an interview with the Quartermaster, who I was certain would allow nothing at all, not even socks. Nobody had a good word for this character.

As usual the working party arrived back expecting me to perform miracles in procuring extras for them so I decided to parade for duty the next morning. When the men found out that I was reporting for duty once more they tried to dissuade me but I had made my decision and found myself back in number four platoon on my way to the Ypres waterworks for a pipe-laying project.

Two platoons were detailed for this work. We arrived in the vicinity of the works round about 9 a.m. on November 10. Our officers met the Royal Engineer officer supervising and a conference took place whilst the rank and file stood at ease waiting for instructions.

The morning was hazy. Practically over our heads was a captive balloon used for observation. Barely discernible in the distance were several more. Suddenly it looked as if three tablecloths were hurled from the passenger basket. They were parachutes: the observer crew had seen something we were not aware of yet – a plane was about to strafe the balloon.

Seconds later a small red tri-plane dived at the balloon from the low clouds. As it neared the pilot opened up with his forward machine gun. The line of spray rising from the ground near us caused us to panic a bit, some men falling flat on the ground. They were ordered up very sharply, and as the diving plane turned in an arc to rise over the balloon again we were ordered to run for safety inside the building. It was difficult to understand the mentality of the pilot. He did not carry any incendiary bullets and right in his sights below him was a couple of hundred troops. He must have had a phobia about balloons.

George was later told that this was von Richthofen – the 'Red Baron'. But he was not particularly known for attacking balloons – he usually had more auspicious targets. If a pilot was going to do this he would normally be armed with incendiary bullets since only these would set the balloon on fire. This form of attack was used over Britain by fighters trying to destroy Zeppelins. The ammunition was known as 'Buckingham' and it was very successful against the hydrogen-filled airships. Inflammable bullets were in fact limited to this sort of operation since it was generally regarded as a violation of the St Petersburg Declaration to use them against human targets. Pilots were allowed to shoot ordinary bullets at the balloon crews.

We were lucky (not a casualty of any description) considering the amount of metal raining from the sky. Quite close at hand was Hell Fire Corner. In one spot adjacent stood a line of twelve or thirteen Lewis guns mounted on tripods. Every aircraft gun locally was blazing away but still this daring man escaped, even with four of our own planes pursuing him over the line back to German-held territory.

After the hubbub had subsided we received a rocket of a dressing-down for falling flat on the ground during the attack. Thinking back over the incident I don't even know what I did at the time. Finally, we got to work on the excavating. The pipes were to be laid six feet below the surface in the direction of Qui Zouave siding and ammunition dump.

Around one o'clock the order was given to break for a short lunch of biscuits, bully beef and an excellent mug of tea made with pure water for a change. We were sitting in groups discussing the eventful morning when a motor cycle dispatch rider appeared. He had news of our unwelcome visitor of the morning: he was Baron Von Richthofen, the German Ace.

In all, he had destroyed five balloons. We continued our trench digging till sundown when the spades were collected and stored, then marched back to our camp at Brielen.

A few days later we were within a short distance of the ammunition dump when suddenly disaster occurred – a shattering explosion sent everything skywards – men, trucks, lorries and stacks of shells and small arms ammunition. Our Unit was again extremely lucky. It was nearing the lunch break therefore we had dug to a depth of four or five feet, this trench providing maximum cover, and we escaped again without casualties.

But it was an entirely different story at the scene of the explosion, approximately one hundred and twenty five men were engaged there at the time and nobody survived. It was a tragic and pathetic sight on the following day when teams of men with four G.S. wagons were gathering up the remains. Close by I saw a man pick up from the ground a steel helmet; it still contained a head.

The water pipe affair petered out after a few days, I think mostly for lack of material, and we were put to work in other places. I was among a party sent on repair work to the notorious Menin Road. Everything seemed to happen along this well-known thoroughfare. It was reputed that the enemy had it registered to the inch. I myself would say to the yard.

But it was one of the British Army's lifelines and the order went out that it had to be maintained at all costs.

About this time (20 November), even Field Marshal Haig abandoned any hope of victory in Flanders. But this made little difference to George and his mates, who were working even harder in the all-embracing mud. The pressure on the Germans was maintained on this date (20 November) with a special offensive in the south of the British sector at Cambrai. A total of 378 tanks achieved a surprise breakthrough against the Siegfried Stellung. However, as usual, early success became bogged down against German defences, and most of the territory gained was lost to a German counter-attack, by the end of the month. Only a tiny part of the Stellung was retained.

The destruction amongst the animals, especially the mules, was very heavy. It was extremely hard work dragging the poor beasts from the fairway and then interring them. They were mainly used as pack animals carrying six or eighteen pounder shells from the dumps to the batteries.

Of course, their riders suffered in this dangerous area. A steady stream of injured were conveyed to probably the largest Casualty Clearing Station, at St Jean. Owing to the early rising necessary on this particular maintenance chore when one party completed a week at it, it was replaced by another. So it came about that a day arrived when I among some dozen or so others received a day's excuse, which was very welcome.

I happened to glance towards the château several hundred yards away and saw a group engaged in a game of football. I, and several others, made our way across, either to watch or participate. I was just a spectator, my feet still being sore.

I got into conversation with one member of the staff belonging to the château. He enquired about what our Unit did and I reciprocated by asking about his work. He answered that he was an actor. I must have given a disbelieving glance in his direction. He came out with the full story: he belonged to a Section which interrogated prisoners when vital information was needed. A prisoner was only required to give his name, rank and number and nothing else.

The actor and five others spoke fluent German. The method they used to loosen the genuine prisoner's tongue was unique. The real prisoner was placed in a passage adjoining the examining office, and either my informant or a colleague would be dragged roughly along and sent flying through the door, which was then firmly closed.

They all then manufactured a series of yells, thumps and bumps. Then the supposed battered prisoner would be dragged through the door again. By the aid of greasepaint and other materials the 'prisoner' would look as if he had undergone a through going over.

This, I think, was known as psychological warfare. The actor hastened to assure me that no one was ill-treated, and that their method very rarely failed in its objective: I made no comment.

8

DECEMBER 1917 – YPRES (ST JEAN/KITCHENER WOOD)

The next day, the first one of December, I was one of a party destined for duty at the St. Jean Casualty Clearing Station. A lorry was engaged to transport us there, so once again we crossed the canal bridge. I mused about what was in store for us on this trip. I had not been to this place previously so everything was new to me. The Red Cross markings at the entrance were very large, and I noticed there was an ambulance train occupying the sidings.

On alighting, a senior NCO started to deploy people to various jobs. I was the last one remaining. He remarked that I was a fresh candidate and I confirmed that it was my first visit. He told me to stay put till he found something for me to get on with. There happened to be a derelict old Belgian farm cart by so I eased my way round to the front of this vehicle with a view to getting the weight off my feet – also a quiet puff at a Woodbine.

George was having a quiet time at the St. Jean Casualty Clearing Station. A Woodbine was the classic 'fag' to soldiers on the Western Front. It was the favoured brand in terms of quality against cost. The tobacco in a Woodbine was mature, something which could not be said about many of the other cheaper brands containing green acrid tobacco which tasted like seaweed. Profiteers made fortunes out of these 'gaspers' – to which they often gave fancy names such as 'White Cloud', Ruby Queen' and 'Red Hussar'. All too often they made up the army ration of cigarettes. There were quality cigarettes much dearer than Woodbines, such as Gold Flake, Players, Three Castles and Virginia or Turkish ('stinkers') or Egyptian. Cigarette prices rose steeply in 1917 due to the U-boat threat, in many cases around 15 per cent. Even a packet of the cheaper cigarettes cost the soldier about half a day's pay (equivalent to a meal or a few drinks). But smoking was addictive, especially when cold and miserable, and when there was a lot of hard work to do. Pre-war non-smokers found it almost impossible to resist the lure of a fag. You could save money by rolling your own with cheap tobacco and Rizla papers. French-grown tobacco was spongy and black and gummed together with spit. Woodbines were often used as currency – say two for a haircut. There was a brisk trade between fags and rum, according to taste. George gave up smoking in 1930 when his great friend, Phillip, died of lung cancer. This was before I was born: I never saw a fag in my father's mouth.

I was successful in this manoeuvre and I got interested in what was happening around. I noticed across the road leading directly into Ypres several large mounds, seemingly covered by camouflaged netting. Just at that moment a short figure came rather stumbling into the entrance drive. As he neared me I noticed something wrong with him. All one side of him was covered in blood. He was wearing a ground sheet cape. He spoke in a Scottish tongue to inform me that an arm had disappeared just above the elbow. I asked him 'You have walked very far?'

The answer and place mentioned in his reply was roughly seven miles away. I queried why walk all that distance with a terrible injury such as that. His reply was 'If I am a walking wounded I'll get a Blighty'. I had no answer to this terrific determination and let him in to receive the kindness and attention he so richly deserved.

Having a 'Blighty' meant being sent back to England for treatment. These combination groundsheets and rain capes were still a novelty in late 1917. If you had been out in the rain you could turn them inside out to use as a groundsheet and vice versa if you had slept on wet ground – almost inevitable in the salient at this time.

Shortly afterwards the Red Cross train I had observed when I first arrived steamed away with its tragic cargo. I was still kicking my heels waiting for orders when another train bustled in. I heard plenty of orders and commands being given and shortly afterwards a long column of smart young Canadian troops marched by where I was standing, past the mounds opposite. I still kept these fine fellows in my sights and noticed that they had been halted some three or four hundred yards past the mysterious mounds I previously spoke about. I saw that they were busily engaged in erecting small, yellow-coloured bivouacs. Knowing the great and pressing need of camouflage, because of the stepping-up of aircraft warfare, I thought these yellow tents extremely unwise and so it proved not so long afterwards.

It was now around eleven o'clock. I saw the RAMC NCO coming in my direction, carrying a carton. He handed it to me saying there were a dozen Machonicie [sic] Rations to heat for my party – one tin between two men. *Maconochie (as it is correctly spelt) has been variously described as a sort of Irish stew in tins, or as a beef stew with potato and mixed vegetables – or, in short, a dinner in a tin. The original beef and vegetable tin was made by Maconochie Bros. of London (at their factory on the Isle on Dogs, where George lived). This company had won 143 gold medals in the food trade. It was obviously a first-rate meal in a tin. But there were many inferior brands which it was unwise to eat in the dark – grisly hashes running with liquid, a piece of rotten meat swamped in rice. Whatever it contained it was better if heated whilst still in the tin (how more men did not go down with metal poisoning is a mystery). Tins of pork and beans exhibited a similar variety in quality. American brands were good, but others had a small lump of pork hidden in a sea of beans, another example of profiteering in Britain.*

I was pleased with this: it was not often that we saw anything like this. These rations were so hard to obtain that they were regarded as luxuries. I was pleased with the fact that I had at last something to get busy on.

When the tins had been heated sufficiently I made it known to the NCO, who gave permission for us to devour this rather substantial repast – at least, it was for us.

Afterwards my comrades went back to their tasks and I took up the same position in front of the aged cart. Since the episode at the waterworks I had developed a tendency of frequently glancing skywards so I was soon made aware of a small plane approaching the Clearing Station. As it flew over the site where the mounds were situated a flare was fired from its cockpit. Then a type of small parachute slowly descended towards the ground. It was quickly retrieved by someone hurrying from what appeared to be a dugout and taken back there. Some five minutes or so later whistles were blown and numbers of men appeared from below ground in the vicinity of the mounds and commenced to strip the camouflage netting, revealing the largest field guns I had ever seen.

At the rear of each of these huge weapons of destruction stood a row of projectiles at least four feet in length. Loading the guns was carried out at lightning speed, and I heard the order 'Fire!' The concussion of this salvo almost knocked me to the ground. I noticed that each gun as it was discharged was propelled backwards to rise upwards on a pair of large timber wedges.

On each gun another enormous shell was being lifted by a davit-type hoist and each disappeared into the breach of a gun followed by a large number of linen bags of cord.

The second order to fire rasped out. This time I was better prepared for the resultant shock. I had put on my balaclava helmet, which nullified the effect on my ears. I was not certain at the time but I had an idea that I saw projectiles disappearing towards the German lines.

The last view was that they looked like cricket balls high in the sky. After firing six salvos the operation ceased and a short time later the battery appeared once again as mounds. Shortly afterwards a member of the gun crews crossed the road to where I was still stationed awaiting instructions.

To allay my inquisitiveness I went up to him using the subterfuge of asking for a light for my cigarette. He complied with this request and started to scan the sky with field glasses. I enquired if trouble was expected: he replied that this was extremely likely considering that over twenty tons of high explosives had just been catapulted on sidings and installations at Roulers, some nine miles away.

He confirmed that it was possible to see projectiles of very large calibre and also hear the report when they detonated. I asked him what was the calibre of the gun he served. The reply – twelve inches.

Shortly afterwards he returned to his underground home near the mounds, leaving me somewhat irked, stationed near an old wagon with nothing to occupy my mind.

Some time later, hoping a mug of tea would be coming my way, whistles started sounding out – aircraft warnings – and low on the horizon I could see the planes approaching. As they neared it appeared the machines were heading directly towards the battery and the Clearing Station behind it.

I noticed that the planes were very large, and counted fifteen. Nothing much seemed to be fired towards them barring their progress. Shortly after they passed over the yellow-dotted encampment of the newly-arrived Canadian troops.

Then a quantity of black lines seemed to drop from the machines. In seconds I knew this was not so: bombs were exploding in direct hits on this camp – dozens of them.

The squadron then passed over the battery and the Clearing Station and wheeled left in the direction of Armentières. The bombing ended when a lorry received a direct hit as it travelled along the road to the lines.

For the next hour there was plenty for me and everyone else available to do. The Canadian Unit had appalling casualties. Everybody was rushing the injured into the Clearing Station – dozens of them. The roadway was red with blood, the surgeons operating non-stop on the poor fellows, and they were immediately placed in the train they had left a short time previously.

Out of five hundred, on a rough estimate, there remained around one hundred or so fit men. Our party was very late in leaving. We received a very generous helping of rum before boarding the lorry taking us back to camp, helping us greatly to ignore the numerous bombs falling near the roadways.

I served with this party for probably a week. The very long working day made it irksome. My special pal, Philip, was moved into a detachment to a camp sited on the Boundary Road. I heard that the work they were involved in was running ammunition to the batteries in the forward area, mostly at night.

It so happened that the medical Corporal informed me that I was due for an inoculation so I had to visit the M.O. whom I had seen after the shell incident along the railway to Flamertinge. I made the trip to get this attention by road, for quite obvious reasons. I had a phobia about railway lines.

He was quite normal as he gave me the injection and asked how I had been faring, and ended by awarding me two days' excuse – very welcome.

Later, meeting the Sergeant Major as I was proceeding to the ablutions shed to carry out some much-needed laundry work, I received permission to visit Boundary Road the next day.

I had received a parcel from home that morning and carried this with me the following day when I travelled across the canal bridge to visit my friend. He was very pleased to see me, and we proceeded to his own private dugout for a natter whilst the water was boiling for tea-making.

He informed me that his main job was waking the members of the various parties so that they arrived on time. I rather think that a reliable alarm clock was needed but I did not pursue this matter.

This camp consisted of dugouts: there were no tents here. After a frugal lunch we decided to nose around the camp surroundings. At one point there was a small brook. Along the banks were a few willow trees and a short while afterward we came back to these and started a small fire. I examined the parcel my mother had sent to me. There were some home cookies, chocolate and (very welcome) some cocoa, which we decided to sample, so Philip went back to his shelter to bring the can.

There was only one water supply – the brook. By this time the fire had burnt low, so taking an old bayonet with me I went to the old willows to prise off some old dead wood or pieces of bark for the purpose of replenishing the fire.

Glancing back at my pal he seemed to be greatly amused for some reason. I found out why when I went to prise some bark from a tree. It was corrugated iron made to look like bark. I walked round the tree. It was a complete phoney.

Behind, low down, was a manhole. This aperture was large enough for me to enter. Inside were ladder rungs about six feet up the walls, which were steel plate made circular, and wide enough for a man's body to move around easily. There was also an oblong aperture six to eight inches wide and three inches in depth – in a nutshell, the complete observation post.

I managed to open this and noticed how the ground sloped away towards the canal bank in the distance. In the meantime, we found an old ammunition box, which was ideal for fuel, and enjoyed some cocoa and cakes.

Around four o'clock I bade farewell to Philip and commenced my journey back to Brielen and finding that I preceded my tent mates made a fire in our homemade stove, and placed some water on to heat up for shaving and other purposes when they turned up.

Parading the following morning (December 11) a list of about twenty names was called by the orderly sergeant to stand on one side while the remainder received instructions for the various working parties. My name was called out and I became aware that we all belonged to the younger element. Two NCOs were among the group, Corporal Salisbury [78628 Corporal Thomas E. Salisbury] and Lance-Corporal Robertson. [There were ten men called Robertson who joined the Labour Corps from the Queen's Regiment – this one is possibly 74727 Corporal Francis A. Robertson.]

We were told to rest up during the day as we were being called very early the next morning. That was the only information about the forthcoming operation we received. Among the selected party including me were three other young fellows and also the Lance-Corporal. Later the two NCOs were seen to leave the camp in the direction of the canal bridge.

After a couple of hours' rest most of us decided we might as well wash and brush up, and whilst we were engaged in the ablutions shed another member of the party came in informing us that he had found out our proposed destination. It was Kitchener Wood, near St Julian on the way to Langemarke [sic] and Paschendaele [sic] – and from what had been gleaned a real hotspot.

The NCOs had been instructed to travel up the duckboards during daylight and receive the engineers' instructions. The prophecy about calling us very early morning was correct: the party was on its way by one o'clock loaded down like pack horses with the stores and equipment needed for the operation.

It was a frosty night but this was infinitely better than the rain. We reached Zouave Road and then took to the duckboard track. We were all pleased with the two NCOs, who were really one of us – no need of any bull of any description.

We kept marching along for a couple of hours, the star shells and verey lights becoming nearer, when a hitch occurred, both NCOs admitting that they had lost the way and did not know which way to proceed. This was not surprising: nighttime was vastly different to daytime, especially in the Salient. It was suggested that we kept our eyes open for any light showing and enquire about direction.

Everyone seemed doubtful about this proposal, but eventually a pair of keen eyes saw a light flare for a second, and we carried on in that direction. When we reached the spot we found it was a member of an artillery battery, who was rather annoyed and startled. He told us to stay put while he brought an officer to interview us. The man came back with this officer, who I noticed was wearing a revolver. After a while listening to the NCOs he seemed satisfied that we were really a lost party and announced that for our own safety we should stay in the battery dugouts till morning light when we could see where we were to go.

After making ourselves as comfortable as possible under the circumstances we were gratified with half a jar of rum sent in by the young gunnery officer. The warming effect of this gift made us drowsy, and, huddled together, we soon dropped off to sleep for a couple of hours after which we were awakened by someone entering with a dixie containing tea.

We soon made ourselves acquainted with this and wondered what was to happen next. Nobody seemed anxious to move us from the warmth and atmosphere of the dugout. Later, the officer appeared. He had a proposition to make, as follows: one of the guns the day before had suffered a near miss and had slid into the resultant shell hole. With our assistance he could get the gun re-sited in position, and in the meantime would provide us with breakfast and, as the mist was thick outside, lend a man to guide us to our destination.

Who could argue with this excellent proposition? Corporal Salisbury covered himself by asking the officer for a formal order, which was given with a pleasant smile, and we settled back once again anticipating the forthcoming meal. After partaking of this we gathered outside to help in recovering and positioning the gun.

Around eleven this task was accomplished and we were on our way to St. Julian under the guidance of a Bombardier. We finally arrived at our destination – Kitchener Wood, consisting of around a dozen or so bare tree trunks. The surroundings were desolate in the extreme: as far as the eye could see stretched a vast array of shell holes.

The 1st Canadian Division had their first experience of the Western Front here when this was a real wood. On 22 April, 1915 they launched a highly courageous counter-attack on well-defended German defences which included a thick hedge interlaced with thick wire. This had to be smashed down with rifle butts as the Canadians were under machine-gun fire. Marshal Foch later called this 'the greatest act of the war'. Seventy-five per cent of the Canadian 10th and 16th Battalions were killed or wounded.

Near the remains of the wood was a ruined stone building and the Corporal told us this had been a police station until struck by a five point nine shell. We reasoned that where one five point nine had landed another one could arrive. We decided on a new dugout. We felt quite comfortable and safe when we were occupying this structure and started a two-shift system on the work allocated to us – namely to dig out a large rectangle for some purpose which we did not know.

There was a clear view down the duckboard track and if someone was seen approaching the field of operation everyone turned to and looked busy. One day, in the dugout, as we engaged in the midday repast, the rattle of machine guns was heard. The man nearest the entrance cautiously peered out and announced that two planes were in combat overhead. We all stayed put till no more gunfire was evident, when we emerged.

We saw some distance away a plane, unluckily one of ours. We did not approach this right away as it was quite possible to see this machine from the enemy's observation balloons.

A short while elapsed, then it was proposed that a couple of men should proceed and have a closer view of the machine. This idea was carried out and it was discovered that the pilot was still in the cockpit. He was unconscious so we all trooped to the plane to get the man free and to safety and medical attention. The nose was half buried in a shell crater, the propeller a write-off.

A few of us secured the tail end of the plane and pulled it level with the ground whilst others were engaged in extricating the pilot. A section of duck-board was brought alongside and the man placed on it, the Corporal remarking that among the injuries the man had sustained a broken leg.

Some eight of the section were detailed to take the man to the hard road, the Corporal going along, to obtain medical assistance.

Next day, a recovery crew from the Royal Flying Corps arrived to dismantle the plane and salvage all the useful remaining parts.

Meanwhile we decided after all that we would turn the ruined police station into something habitable. It could be made larger and materials could be scrounged to increase the number of bunks and other facilities. This privilege was granted and we were also allowed to take turns to stay at the building overnight to continue work on it.

Thus in a short time we were enjoying a great deal more comfort and freedom but unfortunately it was soon apparent that the project at Kitchener Wood was a white elephant mainly due to the amount of water surrounding the spot. As soon as the frozen crust of earth was removed on the first dig of the morning so the men wearing thigh waders sunk slowly in a morass.

It became exhausting work hauling them free. The Corporal was finally informed of the reason for this underground excavation. It was towards ascertaining the vicinity of a long-range gun which was dropping shells on Paris. We never found out about the instruments which were to be employed – some kind of super range-finder in reverse, someone suggested.

George was with his detachment located near Kitchener Wood trying to construct a foundation for some sort of direction-finder to fix on the location of a super-heavy German howitzer. The base would have been surveyed in and a microphone mounted onto it, by listening in on a number of different microphones it was possible to pinpoint the artillery when it shot. Allied soldiers called all these big guns 'Big Berthas' (a whole detachment of the 132 Company sat along the barrel of one of them at Nippes near Cologne after the war). But to the Germans the only real Krupps 'Big Berthas' were the 16.5in M-Gerat howitzers.

A complaint arose about the tea the Corporal was brewing. It was an unappetising colour, a bluey muddy colour. Someone suggested that the Corporal was disposing of the milk to his own advantage. But, being careful (not directly – after all, he was in command), his movements were watched for a few days. The verdict? No blame was attached to him: he had been seen to put the milk in the brew without fail.

Lots of sugar and condensed milk were not the only ingredients added to tea: other less desirable elements also found their way in. For a start the soldiers had to get used to the grease and scum from the cooking pots and dixies in which everything was cooked (there were no tea bags in those days). Moreover, most of the water was conveyed in ex-petrol tins. It was also treated with chloride of lime to guard against disease. After months and years of drinking these cocktails they got used to it: it was not surprising they shoved in a lot of sugar and condensed milk, and rum when it was available.

So this concoction remained a puzzle for a time. After all, the water was coming from the largest shell hole in the vicinity. Chloride of lime had to be added so we concluded this chemical was the cause of the discolouration until a short while later when the enemy almost landed a direct hit on our party and position. The missile landed slap in the crater containing the water supply and the resulting explosion reduced the water supply to a very great extent.

Later that day Corporal Salisbury took the dixie along to the shell hole for a further supply of water for our afternoon brew. Letting out a yell, he dropped the dixie and rushed back to our work side. His eyes were bolting from his head: everyone went to him, wondering what the cause of his consternation was. 'There's a dead man floating in the water!' he exclaimed. When he had regained his composure we all made for the spot. He was correct: the remains of a German soldier were evident on the surface of the water. One wag in the group exclaimed, 'Don't be afraid of that one, Corporal, it's the live ones to be scared of.' Then his face went grey. 'Crikey! You've been getting the water from this crater, haven't you?'

So the secret cause of the nasty-looking tea was revealed. Afterwards, it was decided that water would be brought along with the party each morning by means of several petrol cans and each man with a full water bottle, the water being stealthily obtained during the night from the officers' private tank, and also the NCO Sergeants' mess, also provided with a tank. This led to us really enjoying our cuppas.

We had found out meanwhile that the engineers had decided to carry on after all as the rain had stopped (for a while, anyway) and there was a better bit of ground on the other side of the wood. Shortly after this episode, whilst laboriously shovelling the mud from the new hole I came across the stem of an ornamental pipe, with a tassel attached. I was about to throw this object away when somebody suggested that we might also find the bowl. He was correct: it was unearthed. So during the midday break the cards were cut and the man who found the bowl won and become the possessor of a beautiful Meerschaum Pipe. We all wondered if its original owner was the poor victim we had seen floating in the shell crater.

George was still digging away near Kitchener Wood. Meerschaum is magnesium silicate, mined mainly in Turkey although there was some in Greece, France and Spain. It is a soft material when extracted but hardened under sunlight. As meerschaum matured it darkened in colour to yellow, then orange, then ochre.

We had used a pile of elephant iron (corrugated sheets for Nissen Huts) which nobody seemed to want (it was not wise leaving stuff lying around with Pioneers in the vicinity) on the police station. It was up to us to study our own safety. It had long been realised that the higher-ups had as much consideration for human life as they had for a fly.

The reference to 'Pioneers' is interesting. Infantry Pioneers were not part of the Labour Corps as they consisted of a fully armed infantry battalion attached to each Division and undertook low-level construction. The other 'Pioneers' who were sometimes members of the Labour Corps were initially members of the Royal Engineers (RE) Labour Companies who held the rank of Pioneer (an unskilled Sapper or Private). These RE units became 700 to 711 Companies of the Labour Corps in August 1917.

We now had the manual pumps in operation but still the water gained over our efforts. We were losing thigh waders frequently. If a comrade could not be extricated the straps simply had to be cut and no matter how we pulled and tugged the waders the occasional one was lost, the result being, if no replacements were forthcoming, the loss of an excavator for the time being.

Sometimes after a couple of hours' steady pumping the water from the hole, only two men could commence to remove the remaining mud. The situation was getting hopeless again but we were far from downhearted: no officer was breathing down our necks, nobody seemed to be worried from the engineers' department, so gradually there was more concentration on safety measures round the shelter we had manufactured.

Another job was keeping repaired the duckboards to the hard road because stuff had to be brought along it, about half a mile, bags of cement and more elephant iron, sand and gravel, getting ready for the next stage of operations, if we would ever reach it.

It was suggested to use a couple of the iron sheets, which had a curve at one side, as sledges to put a reasonable load on and tow them towards the site. This idea proved fairly successful.

A Royal Engineer Sergeant did actually turn up on December 17 and we gathered around him to hear the instructions. He seemed pleased at the ingenuity displayed by the idea of using the elephant iron as sledges and suggested that it would be a good thing to bring the rest of the metal and erect it temporarily above ground to use as a store.

It was decided to do this so the remainder of the day was spent in transporting everything to the scene of our future activities. We managed to bolt the sheets together before we left for Brielen so as to keep the cement bags as dry as possible.

The party had to leave Brielen at five o'clock in the morning and was thus given a substantial breakfast before starting on its journey to the duckboards. Corporal Salisbury, who appointed himself site cook, also constructed a lean-to as a cookhouse to enable the preparation of food. We had reasonable shelter from the elements.

But the powers-that-be moved me on the next day. I was now to be saddled with one of the misfits of the Unit. I was sorry for this fellow – Private Sharp [possibly 79987 Private William H. Sharpe – there were twenty-one Privates named Sharp who transferred from the Queen's Regiment to the Labour Corps] – age around forty. This tough life wasn't his scene, at all, continually whining that his three strong and virile brothers were still at home in England. My reply was that I was in the same boat but hoped that my three brothers did not have to come out and experience the conditions we suffered.

This was in conversation with the dreadful Private Sharpe. George's brothers, in order of seniority, were Harry, Tom and Charlie – all younger teenagers. He also had a sister – Cissie. A family with just four children on the Isle of Dogs in those days was rated as a small family. My mother had twelve siblings.

A task for two men at the Ypres waterworks was earmarked for us. At various given spots loads of three-inch pipes were dumped. Our instructions were to carry these and lay them in a straight line alongside the trench which our Unit had dug a while back.

Later, the engineers would follow and connect these lengths before committing them to their resting place in the trench. I hoped that it was not expected that the final filling of the trench was to be accomplished by just two men.

The first day at this occupation was very hard on us. We were plastered with mud up to our necks. The annoying thing was the condition of our greatcoats, soaked in mud and weighing a ton. These were usually used as a third blanket but the state of them made this impossible. So both our overcoats had to be deposited in the ablutions shed overnight.

On the second day I decided not to use the coat but to dress for the occasion with the issue leather jerkin. I encased my legs in half a dozen sandbags. I figured that mud could be cleaned from the jerkin and that the bags could be discarded along with whatever adhered to them.

Sandbags, apart from being filled with sand to pile up in trenches and buildings, tents etc., were also used for a great variety of purposes. A lot of food was carried about in them – if it was wet the bread got soggy! They were the great war version of the plastic bag. There were actually 'Sandbag Clubs' at home where ladies stitched some very ornate samples (which finished up in soaking trenches). The 'Sewing Party' of Godalming sent out 8,000 pretty bags in 1915 – all stolen in transit. A Lieutenant Eberle calculated that he issued 130,000 bags in one period of three weeks in 1916.

I conveyed this idea to Private Sharp but he arrived on parade dressed as usual. The only difference was the extra weight he carried in mud on the greatcoat.

Our pipe humping progressed uneventfully until a sunken road was reached: then we hit trouble. Sharp was at the front end of a pipe and I at the rear. These pipes were carried on our shoulders. He started to pick his steps down the bank of the sunken road when he either stumbled or trod on the end of his rather long coat. The forward end of the pipe thumped down, with the result that Private Sharp was laying in liquid mud, in fact, practically buried in it. I started scraping the filth off, taking hold of the furious mood I was in because he had probably deliberately fallen off the duckboards in order to get off working, in fact, to be sent for rest or even back to Blighty.

Realising that blowing my top wouldn't help the situation I was busy in the task of cleansing the unfortunate fellow when the engineer Corporal arrived on the scene. He stifled his laughter at the appearance of Sharp. He suggested he would help me cart a dozen or so pipes across the roadway then the pair of us, meaning Sharp and myself, could make our way back to an old wrecked house near Hellfire Corner and complete the cleaning up process on Sharp.

We did as the Corporal suggested and I managed to heat a fair amount of water when a roaring fire was started. I spent about an hour making Sharp presentable and came to the conclusion that he should make his way back to camp. It was then around three o'clock. We managed to thumb a lorry which was travelling back to Flamertinge.

Pte Sharp climbed aboard and I proceeded back to the scene of the pipe-laying operation proving, if the engineer Corporal visited again, that I was still present for any allotted task.

Staying till dusk approached, I thought it was time I started on my way back to Brielen. There was no lorry ride for me: arriving fairly late I proceeded to the cookhouse to collect the evening meal. After I had partaken of this repast I made myself as comfortable as possible in my small area of the floor space when an enquiry arose about Sharp.

It gradually dawned on me that he had not arrived back at camp. Eventually the Lance Corporal said that he would have to report him missing and shortly afterwards proceeded to the Orderly Room, taking me along to state what had happened.

By morning there was no sign of Private Sharp so two other men were ordered to the pipe-laying. I received instructions to proceed over the canal bridge and spend all day, if necessary, searching for the missing man.

I arrived back at the camp very late to report that I was unsuccessful and was told to carry on looking the next day. Turning left when I crossed the Yser I made my way to the camp at Boundary Road wondering if Sharp had turned up there, contacting Philip, who was still acting as timekeeper and camp policeman.

He affirmed that he had no knowledge of the missing man but would do his utmost to find him, adding that at the present time there were more important matters in the pipe line to worry over.

During the night the Company had lost four men. It appears they were manning an ammunition train and in the act of crossing a trestle bridge which spanned a swamp the whole structure collapsed into the mire, and out of the party of sixteen and an NCO only twelve of the men had got clear with the Lance Corporal, and at the moment most of the detachment were at the scene looking for the victims and salvaging whatever could be recovered.

Looking through the Commonwealth War Graves Records there are three men listed as having died on 16 January 1918, and only one man from the unit in December 1917. It is believed that George has mixed his dates. This is quite possible when the 'daily grind' was very repetitive. The casualties are believed to have been:

Private Arthur PERKINS, 78954. 132nd Coy, Labour Corps. Age 35. Husband of Ruth Elizabeth Perkins, of 54, Clarendon Rd, Hoe St., Walthamstow, London. Panel 160 and 162A

Private George E. TAYLOR, 79034. 132nd Coy, Labour Corps. Grave no V. C. 46.

Private Charles T. WADE, 79053. 132nd Coy, Labour Corps. Drowned Age 37. Husband of Jessie Elizabeth Wade, of 77, Milton Rd, Stoke Newington, London. Grave no V. C. 47.

They are all buried in Bard Cottage Cemetery or recorded on the Tyne Cot Memorial. A number of other men from different companies in the area are also listed as having died at about the same date, but it is impossible to establish if they were on this train. There is no mention of this in any of the war diaries maintained by Corps HQ.

After my pal had brewed some tea the matter relating to Private Sharp cropped up again. Philip was convinced that a fast one was being worked. He knew that in civilian life Sharp was employed in an office and held a responsible post so he was not so silly as he gave the impression to all and sundry out here.

He was convinced that Private Sharp would arrive back at Brielen in someone's care so in the meantime it was suggested that I stayed on in the dugout, spend the night and then make my way back to the main camp in the morning, thus giving the impression that I had been searching all night.

Leaving Boundary Road very early on my journey back I wasn't able to obtain a lift so the fairly long hike gave an edge to my appetite and so I collected a breakfast meal before departing to the Orderly Room. After hearing of my unsuccessful efforts. I was told to deputise for a man who had accidentally fallen into a shell hole and arrived back to camp soaked to the skin.

The party he was a member of was proceeding to Kitchener Wood to dismantle and convey all useful materials to the hard road to enable them to be picked up by lorry and conveyed back to engineers' stores. Evidently, the Kitchener Wood project had been abandoned.

It was well in the morning before I arrived at St. Julian to find the elephant iron shelter had already been dismantled and the curved sections were being prepared for use as sledges to convey the hand pumps and other collateral back over the mud.

I enquired how the man had managed to stumble into the shell hole. It appears that after the party had left the Zouave Road to proceed along the duckboards it was still fairly dark. A German plane arrived overhead and at intervals dropped six bombs. All were near misses and penetrated so far into the deep mud before exploding that the only injury suffered by the party was the one when the man who was looking backwards and upwards stumbled and fell into the deep shell crater alongside the duckboards and received a soaking. We all worked with a will to get the job completed and make an early start back to camp. All the stores were on the hard road by around three o'clock. The Corporal in charge thought that the daylight would allow us to follow the road back to the canal bridge (or so he had been informed), so this route was tried and was proved to be quite good, and so we were all able to visit the ablutions and wash and shave etc., also to start the fires going in the tent stoves – which would be much appreciated by the latecomers.

It was now approaching the end of the year. The Company was found a great deal of employment. One regular chore was carrying out repairs on the Menin Road. My pal's prediction regarding the missing Private was correct. He had been found with supposed loss of memory and was brought back by the Military Police. He had been wandering around calling at various posts, mostly artillery positions. He seemed to have received a meal before leaving each place.

He appeared to be nice and plump. He must have dismounted from the lorry before it reached the canal bridge, probably during a traffic jam, and made off in the meantime.

He was confined to camp and ordered to assist in the cookhouse. One thing I desired was that our paths were kept that way – apart. Finally, Christmas Eve was here with us: a large party had been employed at St. Jean Clearing Station and we struck lucky in that lorry transport had been provided to carry us back to camp.

We were all were rather sad – one of the Company had been killed by shrapnel, leaving a wife and six children in England. In the lorry I was travelling in, the conversational subject was what kind of a Christmas we were likely to experience. One man who had been badly injured in 1916 and had been transferred to our unit recalled the fraternisation truce of an earlier Christmas when the front line troops of both sides had proceeded over the top of the trenches, exchanged cigars, rum, schnapps and other good things, singing carols together and playing soccer.

There is only one man from 132 Company listed as having died on or about this time:

78652 Private Charles G. Barwick. He is buried at Mendinghem Military Cemetery – Poperinge, West-Vlaanderen grave VI. BB. 29.

The aftermath arising from the High Command of both sides was fury with the knowledge that such unwarranted actions might cause the early cessation of hostilities on the Western Front. The outcome of this discussion was almost a disaster. One of the group riding on the lorry formed the impression that what he had been listening to was actually on the agenda for the following day!

For a long time now, air activity had greatly increased, and the rank and file had to be more and more cautious at night about fires or naked lights.

Our evening meal was no different to what we usually received – a portion of alleged beef, two potatoes boiled in their jackets, some rice and raisins, and probably a pint of tea with the allotted ration of rum added.

Later, the Orderly Officer called at each tent with two of the cooking staff to serve the pudding. It was not so much pudding as conserve because it couldn't be sliced. It was dished out with the aid of a spoon.

After this repast there was a faint sign of merriment in the air. We were all rather pleased that no actual work was to take place outside the camp tomorrow and that the call to the cookhouse was to be the late hour of eight o'clock.

But, a little later, the fellow who had this idea in his mind – that hostilities had ceased for the time being – decided that the fire in his tent could be taken outside and brightened up. The hot coals were in an old bucket. Putting a cloth around the handle of this he carried it out and started whirling round and round his head to get the heat up.

He got the heat up alright! Within a minute or two aircraft warning whistles were sounding out and we were awoken from a deep slumber by bullets whizzing through the tent over our heads.

We dare not move. What was going on? After just a few seconds (it seemed a lot longer) the firing stopped and we lay there literally stunned and scared out of our wits.

The silence was deafening. Then came slight sounds of movement from outside. We started stirring but were careful to keep our heads well down. I was first to crawl out: other dim figures were crawling out from tents and there was some shouting from the officers' tents. It seemed we had been strafed by a plane.

Later the story became clearer: somebody – no one ever found out precisely who it was – had taken a fire outside his tent and buffed it up. The embers of it were still clear to see: somebody had tried to celebrate Xmas with a cheery fire! An enterprising enemy pilot had seized the opportunity to have a go.

We were lucky once more – only four men wounded, including the lovable (some say) Private Sharp. Was it him that took out the fire? Phil had said that Sharp did have a responsible job in civvy street – how could he be so stupid? Perhaps, though, he was being clever? Anyway, he got a Blighty one so draw your own conclusions!

The next task after the plane had reversed its route was to put things in order again. Our tent had only received four small holes but the pole had been forced through the top. This was soon repaired and we were soon replacing the sand-bags and other protectives in the circle outside. [This was normal practice as it protected the men inside from shrapnel.]

We soon got back to normal. Private Waterlow [79059 Private George H. Waterlow] went off to collect two Xmas pudding tins from the nearby Royal Field Artillery canteen. He arrived back with these tins full of rather strong ale and fragments of the puddings still adhering to the walls of the receptacles, adding extra body to the beverage.

So by and large Christmas had really commenced: as promised there was very little to do on this day and a little extra in the way of luxuries came from the store – an orange for each man and a few dates and chestnuts. The latter were roasted by us.

There was no work for George and his comrades and they received an orange and a few dates and chestnuts, which was a lot better than the fare of Rifleman Eccles of the 7th Battalion, the Rifle Brigade, who spent four days in a hole on Passchendaele Ridge over Christmas. The South Midlands Field Ambulance had roast pork and 'all the trimmings', plum pudding, apples, oranges, wine and extra cigarettes.

Boxing Day saw a return to the round of commitment once again. One new and important one was in the pipeline: the Menin Road was becoming increasingly dangerous and the powers-that-be decided that a subway was to be constructed under it.

Although the 3rd Battle of Ypres had dwindled to a halt in November the area was still lethal, especially on the road between Ypres and Menin, closely registered by the enemy artillery. The second stage of the battle in September had straddled this roadway.

I wondered – after the failure of the project at Kitchener Wood – how they expected us to dig that in the slimy mud!

An entrance was actually started but before long, owing to the increasing proficiency of aerial photography, an enemy plane carrying a particularly heavy and special bomb completely obliterated the work already accomplished.

George in Cologne in 1919.

The opening page of George's diary.

At the beginning of March 1917 I was
approaching My nineteenth Birthday which was the tenth of
April. little did I know that I was to celebrate this event
on the Somme, I was employed as a Docker in the South
West India Docks mostly discharging sugar from Cuba, this
was extremely heavy labour. being tall I was a back lifter
in a piling squad. consisting of five men, although I
was a near six footer my weight was 9 stone 2 lbs. I gradually realised that I was being dehydrated though exces-
sive hard Work and lack of Nourishment so the time had
arrived when I decided to alter these curcumstances —
On the first Monday of March a fresh consinment of sugar got
through the balmarine Blockade. the squad was busily engaged
piling the heavy bags. after lunch which was not a lot. I
enraged the largest lout of the four. at least twice my
weight. He was under the mistaken impression that He could
misname me with impunity. I answered this character so effectively

A view of the trenches.

Building a light railway. (© IWM Q4614)

A square meal – bully beef and hard tack biscuits. (Horace Bruckshaw)

A German dugout in 1917.

There was a great demand for rum. (© IWM Q 4619)

Captain Albert Ball by his SE5, April 1917.

The YMCA hut in Sailly-sur-la-Lys. (Henry Ogle)

Chinese labourers at work in Boulogne, August 1917. (© IWM Q2700)

Railway gun 'Cyclone', September 1917.

Crossing the Ypres–Yser Canal past a sea of mud in 1917. (© IWM Q5714)

Balloons go up.

A 12-inch howitzer is prepared for action.

A Gotha GV bomber.

A 'tree' observation post.

Ypres mud, 1917. This is a road! (Australian War Memorial, negative E01318)

Destroyed British tank near Cambrai in 1918.

A Christmas concert in 1918. (© IWM Q8377)

Marching into Cologne, December 1919.

British tanks by Cologne Cathedral, 1919.

The end of George's memoir.

Sundays, the weeks passed by and the old members of the Queens original Rank were being demobilised in increasing numbers and early in November my turn to go arrived on the third. I journeyed down the Rhine to Rotterdam on the very vessel I had been employed on for quite a time earlier in the year, the next day survived an extremely rough passage across the North Sea to Harwich and arrived at Crystal Palace where I spent the night and was granted Demobilization leave the next morning November the fifth, 1919 – with the princely sum of nineteen pounds in my pocket –

A Labour Company returns to camp after a hard day's work. (© IWM Q2992)

George in the 1920s.

9

JANUARY–FEBRUARY 1918

On Sunday, January 20 our camp was visited by a senior member of some kind of welfare organisation. He took a dim view of the fact that the dug-out interior of the tents were deficient of wooden floors. He promptly ordered that this defect was to be remedied.

Also, an old brewery in Poperinge was taken over by the military to be converted into a bathing and cleansing station. This idea was not very effective. I amongst fifty other rank and file were marched to this building, only spending a few minutes in the hot water in the former beer vats before being raucously ordered out.

We were then handed fresh clothing, which had been fumigated. The failure of this excellent idea was that the garments never fitted and a few days later became as heavily populated as our original clothing. The trouble was the lack of time allowed for the operation thinking of the numbers of troops needing this service.

This referred to lice, one of the blights of a soldier's life on the Western Front. It was hoped that the other horror – rain – would drown the lice but in fact they liked wet weather. They could be burnt out of seams with fags or matches or lighters. It was more tedious but cheaper and more successful to crunch them between finger and nail. Soldiers could sit around nattering whilst the 'chats' were despatched, hence the origin of the word 'chatting'.

Remedies such as Harrison's Pomade had to be smeared over affected parts but it was as thick as engine oil (more patent cures are described in my book *A Bloody Picnic: Tommy's Humour 1914-18*, 2010). The most effective cure was to place offending garments on ant-hills.

On Friday, February 1 some time later the promised floorboards were delivered and we spent time in fitting this luxury but there was a snag: it took a time to get used to laying on something hard. Beforehand the earth was imprinted with the contours of the sleeping men so that once an individual settled in these impressions he was fairly comfortable.

10

MARCH 1918 – BARLY

At some stage 132 Company moved from Ypres southwards, towards Arras. There are no records of when this happened, but other records suggest it occurred after the start of the 21 March offensive (the Kaiserschlacht). General Gough's 5th Army had just taken over a large portion of the French Front and the new area required considerable labour to 'bring it up to standard'. When 132 Company was moved to support the 3rd Army at Barly (North of the main offensive), west of Arras, this proved to be the pivotal point of the Michael Offensive, part of the Kaiserschlacht.

However, such discomfort was nothing compared to what was in store for us in March when after a terrific bombardment lasting the whole night through the enemy broke through, using the forces which had originally been engaged on the Eastern Front. It transpired afterwards that this reputed number of one million had been training with this objective for months.

A million men had been transferred from the defunct Eastern Front and General von Ludendorff considered that the only chance of victory was to launch a massive offensive before the Americans arrived in strength. The great bulk of this attack was against the British lines – which had taken over another 42 miles from the French – to beyond the River Oise. This extended area was not as well defended as the rest of the line, making it particularly vulnerable to the German offensive, although the whole line was in some jeopardy. The initial assault occurred well south of Ypres but diversionary attacks were launched on the Ypres Salient in order to stop reinforcements moving south.

It was soon realised that our camp had to be abandoned and soon the Unit was making tracks towards Poperinge. A lot of equipment had to be left behind (and the floorboards). We only took immediate stores of food and cookhouse equipment. Fortunately, the detachment at Boundary Road had earlier in the year rejoined the main Company at Brielen.

Arriving at the railhead at Poperinge the order to fall out was given and the main topic of conversation was what was happening in the Salient and where we were bound.

At last the latter query was answered: our directive was towards a line of long trucks on narrow gauge lines. We were ordered to climb aboard and after various groups had loaded on goods and chattels we steamed away south along one of the craziest lines I have ever seen. It seemed to weave about in all directions.

Sometimes we moved through beautiful terrain, especially the hilly districts. Most of the time during the journey we were in sight of the observation balloons and occasionally were greeted with one of the long-range shrapnel shells of the high explosive variety.

Travelling along till dusk there was still no sign of any halt being made to the trip. Gradually a bright full moon appeared and also the enemy's night fliers. Finally, near Arras, we were compelled to stop in the midst of what appeared to be a large orchard. It was around one o'clock in the morning and to our surprise one of the trucks contained replacement tents for the fifty or so we had been forced to leave behind. These were evened out amongst the men, usually sixteen to a tent.

We were ordered to disperse in the orchard whilst the C.O. and officers reconnoitred the surroundings. Eventually, a satisfactory position was discovered and the tents erected in very quick time.

But one more chore had to be achieved before we were allowed to lie down and take a few hours' welcome repose – the interior earth had to be removed and placed against the railings outside for protection against bomb fragments. This naturally caused a grumble amongst the men but the reminder of the episode at Christmas soon stifled the moans.

Reveille was at six o'clock, then the orders were to board the train right away, and our journey continued, uninterrupted for at least a couple of hours.

One welcome point was clear to everyone – we seemed further away from the battle zone. [They had been moving West, away from the line.]

Transport for luggage and part kit was awaiting at this halt. We were mustered and marched away in a very short time, accompanied by only one vehicle carrying the cookhouse equipment. Probably around six miles were covered before a halt was ordered.

Then trouble occurred owing to some men not obeying instructions. The kitchen boilers were set up and a pleasant anticipation of a forthcoming mug of hot tea was apparent. Each platoon was ordered to pass by a boiler in single file and empty their water bottles into it. All men without water had their names and numbers recorded.

Back in rank again iron rations had to be inspected. A large proportion of these iron rations were not produced and a second list of offenders was jotted down to receive disciplinary punishment at a later date.

The troops were not allowed to start on their iron (emergency) rations (also the term for enemy bombardments) without an officer's permission. They were contained in something which resembled a horse's feed bag. There was usually a 12oz tin of bully beef, hard biscuits, tea and (normally) sugar. Some also had a piece of cheese or a cube of meat extract. Permission to eat iron rations was granted, according to a platoon commander of the 9th Battalion of the Royal Sussex Regiment, when 'your belly button hits your backbone and your hip bones stick out of your trousers'. The illicit consumption of iron rations was especially prevalent during the headlong retreats of March and April 1918.

We were then allowed to fall out. All eyes were interested in the boilers hotting up when a motor cycle dispatch rider appeared and handed a message to the C.O. and within minutes the Company was formed up once more, the boilers emptied and loaded on transport, and we resumed our travels once more. Only this time we zig-zagged back north. No one seemed inclined to burst forth into one of the popular marching songs prevailing at the time. We were led by the C.O. on a charger, the first instance of him being mounted. The general agreement was that we were destined for a very long march.

On we went for fifty minutes and then fell out for ten minutes of rest. Back on the road once more the same procedure was repeated. After the third fall-out, as we resumed our progress, it was noticed that a few of the ranks were getting distressed and falling out without waiting for the order at a given time of fifty minutes.

This was standard 'March Routine' but it must be remembered that the Labour Corps were all medically downgraded due to age or physical ability, so this march must have been most distressing.

N.C.Os were ordered to wait back and collect these stragglers. Suddenly we marched into a heavy rain storm, and as we were equipped with a combined ground sheet and cape we unpacked and donned these useful articles, only to be barked at by the C.O. to take them off and repack them into our kit.

The reason given? No orders had been issued to put the capes on. But what was thought to be the real reason was that the old fellow's trench coat was in the baggage following on and he wasn't able to wear it.

The result of this stupid restriction was that everyone received a soaking. On receiving the command for the next fall-out we were getting extremely distressed and miserable, wondering what was in store for us all. There was no respite until about six o'clock in the evening when an old prisoner of war camp came in sight.

POWs were not to be employed within the range of enemy guns. As a result of the collapse of the British Front POW camps and camps for civilians (such as the Chinese Labour Corps) were evacuated.

As we entered this it seemed we had reached our objective. The unfortunate stragglers were arriving at various intervals. The main topic of conversation was the behaviour of the C.O.

It was extremely late before we finally settled down for the night. A meal of sorts had been provided and we were fairly comfortable in Nissen huts. But it was hardly daylight when reveille blared out. After a meagre breakfast each man took possession of a spade, and led by the second in command, we marched over to a nearby ridge and shortly met up with a group of Royal Engineers.

We realised from the line of white tape stretching out of sight that a defensive trenching operation was to be undertaken. As each man's section was pegged the work commenced.

The work involved building new reserve trenches, and some Labour Corps units were now issued rifles to enable them to defend the Reserve Line. By 1918 the Labour Corps generally operated a 'Task Work' system and each platoon/section was allocated an amount of trench to dig. Once the unit had done its allotted task, work was over. Obviously during the German offensive men were kept working.

We were told to break off for half an hour midway through the day. But all there was available to eat were some hard biscuits. On returning to our new HQ at dusk a mess of thin stew was available for supper.

11

APRIL 1918

So we laboured on, and came the day the famous 'Order of the Day' issued by Earl Haig was made known to all and sundry (April 11). The next day was occupied on a very hard slog at trench digging on little sustenance, and this was repeated till the distance between the operation and the camp became so great that a move was ordered – Hazebrouck was approached.

The Order concluded: 'There is no other course open to us but to fight it out. Every position must be held to the last man: there must be no retirement. With our backs to the wall, and believing in the justice of our cause, each one of us must fight on to the end. The safety of our homes and the freedom of mankind alike depend on the conduct of each one of us at this critical moment.'

Rank and file never knew how near the Germans got, and how near to disaster we were. We were receiving infantry training, each man was issued with a rifle and bayonet and each day after we had partaken of the evening meal we learnt how to lacerate bags of straw with a fixed bayonet.

The Labour Corps was initially unarmed, partly due to the time involved in training the men and keeping them trained. With the German 'breakthrough' a number of companies, in the 1st and 3rd Armies, were partly armed from 15 April 1918. Initially the aim was to arm all the men of the Labour Corps, but so many weapons had been lost in the German attack that only some men were armed. Later some of these armed companies were re-titled 'Garrison' Companies and at the end of May 1918 they were all transferred to the Infantry. They became, amongst others, the 23rd Battalion Lancashire Fusiliers and 25th Battalion Kings Royal Rifle Corps. Eventually all Labour Companies had at least one armed platoon. George and company had zig-zagged north again towards Hazebrouck. The Germans threatened to break through to the coast (Hazebrouck was only about 35 miles from Boulogne). Not only were the Labour Battalions and Companies ready to fight, they were also digging extensive reserve trenches. Further south, the Germans advanced more than 20 miles, capturing Messines and Armentières, and reached 20 miles from the coast south of Hazebrouck. George and his comrades were in serious trouble. But the enemy advance soon lost its momentum as the Tommies fought back tenaciously. The only really extensive incursion was in the south of the British sector where the 3rd and 4th Armies were swamped as Bapaume and Péronne fell and Amiens was under threat for a time. But even here German power waned: Paris was never in danger.

Once a week we were taken to a firing range to aim at the circles painted on biscuit tins and endeavouring to score bulls on these. At least some succeeded whilst others even fired over the rear of the range itself and were very quickly seen to by the officer in charge.

At least the weather was now much kinder, the evenings much lighter. The Company was housed once more under canvas. The trench-digging was unending but there was no question that it was needed. In all it ultimately must have reached hundreds of miles. On one occasion later in April we were engaged on a section at a place called Loevre. It was very low-lying ground – a marshy swamp. Where this was very wet the trench had to be constructed above ground by means of posts hammered into the surface, and then clad with hurdles secured by means of wire.

It was while we were occupied at this particular spot that we witnessed the passage of a complete French Army. The whole day this great concourse of men and arms passed by us as we worked. It was a great and reassuring sight, especially as the men seemed so bright and cheerful as they greeted and waved to us.

But now another calamity was approaching the forces: it was an epidemic known subsequently as Spanish flu, a truly horrible malady. A great percentage of the troops became victims and a large number of fatalities occurred. Our own roll call diminished daily as the men were stricken and carried off to makeshift centres.

'Spanish Flu' (March 1918–20) as it became known infected some 500 million people, of whom between 50 and 100 million died (it is impossible to establish an exact number particularly as all the combatant powers censored the casualty lists). This is more people throughout the world than were killed in the war. There are various theories as to its origin, even one suggesting it started in the main British Reinforcement Camp at Étaples with a virus spread from poultry to pigs and then humans. It is also argued that adult deaths were greater due to the malnourishment caused by the war.

I estimate that around twenty-five per cent of the Unit contracted this illness but the remaining men were expected to complete as much trenching as the company excavated while at full strength.

Every day the sun was disappearing when we arrived back to settle down for the night. More often than not the enemy planes were flying overhead, and an added nuisance was a shell arriving every ten minutes or so and landing in the wrecked village just beyond the camp. The shell was landing in the same area all the time, thus proving that its sole purpose was to keep us awake and thus decrease our efficiency.

On 18 April the Company re-joined the 2nd Army at Blaringhem, 2 miles east of Hazebrouck, and were involved in digging the GHQ Defence Line.

Hazebrouck was a favoured spot for our trenching operation as the digging of fortifications through wrecked rows of shops enabled us to unearth the original stocks – all kinds of luxury food and goods had been buried under the ruins.

Of course, salvaging and collecting these articles was not allowed officially but a secret supply of tins and bottles found a welcome haven in our camp near St. Sylvestre Capel [north of Hazebrouck].

But the time came when I contracted my dose of the Spanish influenza. At that time a line of defence trenches were being excavated through an area known as the Forest of Nieppe. The Unit was still very much below strength and each man was still getting an abnormal amount to accomplish.

The area was extremely low-lying and soggy. One day I had been toiling away for an hour or so when instead of a spadeful of muddy clay I unearthed a large piece of fur. A little later it dawned on me that below was the carcass of a horse. The air around it was unbearable. I contacted the Sergeant, whose only comment as he tapped my gas mask was 'What are these for, boy?!' So, donning the mask, I resumed the disagreeable chore, and so did the men who were digging on either side of my position. It soon became apparent that the defunct animal had been of the heavy draft breed: it was enormous and had been interred across the line taken by the trench.

In a little while the eye pieces of the mask became steamed up and I was forced to remove it, carrying on excavating and trying to hold my breath at the same time.

I arrived back at camp feeling woozy and completely under the weather. I was unable to eat and retired to bed as soon as possible.

Next morning one of my fellow occupants of the tent came in with the astounding news that the bread ration that day was half a loaf for each man. This phenomenon had never occurred previously. But I remained unmovable for the simple reason that I was too ill to rise from my bed. At the thought of eating I had to refrain from vomiting.

'How many to a bun?' was the daily question in camp (and in the trenches). A customary ration of 16oz (half a 2lb loaf) became common in 1917 (a reduction from 18oz earlier). Quite often the ration behind the front line fell below the standard issue, so if George had been getting more than half a loaf he had been faring well. Extra bread from local sources was usually expensive and in very short supply in 1918.

The outcome of all this was a visit from the medical Corporal, who ordered me to lay quiet. Later, a Crossley ambulance carried me and several others to a Casualty Clearing Station, which I found out later was at St. Omer.

George had caught Spanish flu. Casualty Clearing Stations (CCS) were further back from the front line than Aid Posts and Field Ambulances. The CCS would either get the wounded soldier back to duty or pass him on to a Base Hospital.

During the night I remember some kind of bang in the head. Next morning it was discovered that I had experienced a haemorrhage from the nose which left me in such a mess that the bedding had to be changed.

12

MAY 1918

It was nearly three weeks before I was allowed to leave hospital. During the first fortnight I partook of no solid food whatsoever, just liquid. As companions I had two other members of my Unit. We were all so weak that walking to the railhead was a great effort. To our consternation, when we arrived at the site of our camp there was nothing nor anybody to greet or receive us.

We sank to the ground, thoroughly deflated. We realised we had to remove ourselves from this spot before dark so we decided to make tracks to the railhead and contact the Railway Transport Officer, who would have knowledge of our Company's departure and ultimate destination.

As we staggered away from the deserted site, destined for a reluctant trip of several miles to the railhead, I smiled faintly inwards at our desire to get back to our Unit and once again hear the raucous bark of the Old 'So-and-so', more generally known as 'No. 1'.

We arrived at the railhead and it took a while to contact the R.T.O. He had retired to his well-fortified Nissen hut for some time. As a rule, this species were a little hard to get on with. But things were made easy by the fact that the weakest one of the trio of callers collapsed in his doorway.

We were facetiously asked what strong drink he had imbibed but it did not take long to explain the situation, and the officer proved to be quite human. He handed us over to the care of an NCO, who took us to a nearby bunker-cum-dugout, furnished with some half a dozen chicken-wire bunks. He later supplied us with tea and food and offered the information that the details of the rest of our journey could wait until the morning.

We were soon asleep, and after breakfast around nine o'clock instructions to stand by and wait for the arrival of a troop train were issued. Some time later an asthmatic old locomotive towing a string of box trucks steamed into the siding.

We were given the news that our battalion had travelled southwards to a place called Aveluy. This place was near the River Ancre, a tributary of the Somme. Occupying the truck was an assortment of men all returning to their Units. When we climbed aboard the complement was around fifteen. Usually twice that number were crammed into this space so everyone was allowed a fair amount of room.

The unit had moved on 7 May 1918. This meant that 132 Company were still in the thick of the battle. Albert, just a few miles south of Aveluy, was still in enemy hands. But by this time the front had stagnated: any threat to Amiens had significantly declined.

It was interesting to hear the various topics and conversations of this assorted group. Several had been inside the Salient at the time of the great breakthrough and had witnessed some atrocious behaviour inflicted on helpless men, which led them to avow that their future behaviour would be similar – total warfare.

One man recounted an incident during an attack near Albert on a trench held by Germans. One of them managed to mow down nine of his comrades before extending his arms in the air. The treatment meted out to the German probably crippled him for life, that is if he lived. He was practically kicked out of sight.

On Thursday, May 16 we met up with our Company once again and were booked sick to visit the Medical Officer, who ordered one week's excused duty. Not much task work seemed to be taking place and some of the men were engaged in fishing in the local river, and, surprisingly enough, catching some fish.

This was at Aveluy on the River Ancre, a tributary of the Somme. A more widespread and popular pastime was throwing grenades into rivers, streams and canals in order to stun the fish and pick them out of the water. This carried a rather stiff penalty of Field Punishment No 1 for 28 days (you were tied to a wagon wheel or post or gate for several hours at a time). It didn't seem to deter the men from doing it.

A request was made by the Sports Officer for anyone interested in cricket to forward their name. Very few responded so he came rooting around for volunteers. I was approached and after remarking that I had never played the game he answered 'Good – everyone has to begin' and my name went into the book as a volunteer for practice.

A wicket was subsequently prepared and a scratch game arranged. Of course, the equipment was not of first-rate order, especially the leg guards. My turn came to wield the bat. I had begun to enjoy the game and exercise and faced up to the Sports Officer.

His first delivery struck me an almighty blow in the left thigh and then four more in succession hit me. The sixth missed me and flattened the wicket and I was helped from the scene.

Back at the billet I was still rubbing my bruised thigh and remarked to all and sundry how such a slight man could hurl a ball with such speed and power. A couple of the men asked 'You don't know who that is?'
'Of course I do, 'I replied, 'he's our Lieutenant'. 'But you don't know that he's an amateur pace bowler for Essex at home, do you?'

This information ended all my future aspirations for playing cricket. Later that evening I received a visit from Lieutenant F.G. Dodridge. He was concerned that I was practically lamed and said that he had only bowled around half pace.

Inwardly, I said to myself, 'You won't ever get any opportunity of bowling at me again, not even underarm.'

His last remark before leaving was, 'You'll have to move around a bit otherwise the leg will go rigid. I'll send you a walking stick – that should help.'

I also said something but made quite sure that it escaped his hearing.

13

JUNE 1918

On June 1 a wire for assistance came from No. 1 Air Depot up north, situated at St. Omer: a hurricane force storm had created havoc with the canvas and fabric covering of numerous hangars. No. 1 T.D., under the direction of Lt. Cousins, were sent for to put matters right.

Four lorries were put at our disposal and soon the column was on its way north. The time occupied on this journey of around a hundred miles was five or six hours. We were allowed only one short break, arriving at the depot about six in the evening.

Whilst the Lieutenant made enquiries the main body stood at ease. There was a need to relieve myself so I asked permission of the sergeant to fall out to visit the little hessian room.

As I emerged after the visit, I was confronted by a young staff officer. 'Halt!' he screamed, glaring at me and pointing to a notice that in my hurry I hadn't observed and which said 'Officers Only'.

Over his shoulder he barked 'Sergeant, fall in two men and arrest this man.' The sergeant did his best to mollify this upstart. My offence was clearly an oversight on my part but, like Shylock, he wanted his pound of flesh.

So after handing over the reins to the corporal the sergeant started a long trek all over this vast area to find out where the local cells were situated. But he obtained no satisfaction wherever he enquired until someone had the bright idea of saying, 'Lock him up for the night and bring him in front of his officer in the morning.'

In the meantime there was a pressing need for rations to be issued for fifty men. I got the lion's share to carry – a large sack containing the bread. By this time heavy rain was falling and I received the rather silly order to keep the bread dry.

The evening ended with the desperate criminal being locked up securely for the night in some form of stable – very annoyed and damp. Breakfast was brought to me in the morning around seven thirty and the jailer informed me that Lieutenant Cousins would see me at eight o'clock.

'Will the firing squad be ready?' I enquired which brought a smile to the man's face as he left the building. At the appointed time I was taken in to get the verdict from our own commander, Mr. Cousins. In civilian life he was only interested in workers, and after listening to the sergeant's account of my lapse he asked 'What sort of worker is this man?'

'He's a very good worker,' was the reply.

'Well, put him to work,' said the Lieutenant, and shortly, with skeins of twine, needle and canvas patches, I was on my way to join the rest of the detachment, from whom I received quite an ovation.

Our sojourn at St Omer lasted only a week and we were quite relieved to shake off the dust of this place from our feet. We were well looked after as regards food and shelter but the red tape was greatly overdone. To our surprise, instead of journeying back to the Albert sector again the lorries made for St. Sylvestre Capel.

The remainder of the Company was already back at the camp. After securing my place in the tent and putting my equipment in its right place I made my way to see my pal, Philip, who filled in details of the happenings of the past week. There had been marching on three of the days on the trek north.

At one point, near Gouzencourt, they had to march past a dreadful scene: a complete German battery had been obliterated by bombs. It was a tangled mass of men, horses and guns spilled over the side of the road. Not even the little mascot dog had escaped.

Now that plenty of reserve trenches had been excavated and the roads around seemed in good shape the order of the day seemed to be plenty of spit and polish, drill and long marches, particularly around the Hazebrouck area.

We began to wonder whether these marches had a twofold objective: it appeared that the Allied lines around this area were very thinly held.

By stretching the platoons (and other Companies were doing likewise) this probably created an illusion of strength in reserve in the rear areas.

In fact, the brasswork, rifles etc. were so polished that the general feeling was that the Boche would do something about it, and, sure enough, he did. Besides rifles and side arms we were now equipped with two machine guns, swivelled and adapted for use against air attack. All ranks received instructions in the use of these efficient weapons. [Lewis guns were first issued as anti-aircraft weapons to the Labour Corps in May 1918.]

The Company was passing through a partly derelict farmhouse when several faint pops were heard overhead. In no time the road was deserted and the diving pilot had nothing in his sights to fire at. His practice bursts had been a little premature, and as for getting the Lewis gun in action it was buried inside the old farmhouse under a score or more of prone men.

The disappearing German zoomed away into the hazy sunshine. But this was a near disaster for the Company and for a short interval the road marches were discontinued. Next morning it was decided to send the two guns to the vicinity of the old farmhouse in case the German plane decided on another visit.

A section of helpers went along to help and establish concealed barricades and other advantages. But the project proved fruitless and the party arrived back in camp in time to line up for a pay parade. At the same time each man was ordered to place his cap badge on one table and then proceed to another table and take possession of a badge of a different design.

On formation of the Labour Corps (April 1917) units continued to wear their original infantry badges. New personnel joining would have worn the Royal Coat of Arms (the General Service badge). In October 1918 'The Labour Corps Badge' consisting of a rifle, shovel and pick piled together with the motto LABOR OMNIA VINCIT (Work conquers all) was approved but this would take months to issue. The badge George would have received is the General Service Badge.

We had come to know that our old badge was very well-known affectionately in all spheres as the 'Mutton Lancer', really the figure of a ram with a lance sloping against its shoulder.

This was the Queen's famous cap and collar badge – the Paschal Lamb with lance and flag, perhaps originally a Christian emblem in the fight against the infidel Moors in Tangiers (the regiment was formed in 1661 to garrison this town).

The new badge was the Royal Coat of Arms – the Lion and the Unicorn. At the base were laurel leaves. Some wag amongst us remarked that a famous maker of jam used this identical group of animals in an advert with the words 'By Appointment to his Majesty the King'.

Later we discovered that no longer were we to be known as the 24th Battalion Queen's Royal West Surreys but the 168th Labour Company. We felt completely deflated with this event.

The Company number is wrong, it was 132 Company, and the change in title should have occurred in April 1917 (fourteen months earlier!). This shows opposition to change amongst all ranks. A soldier did not want to be a member of a 'Labour Corps' and as such when the war was over their medals would have been marked 'Queen's Regt' and their graves would have shown their original cap-badge. When the Labour Corps was re-formed in October 1939 for the Second World War, it was entitled the Auxiliary Military Pioneer Corps, later shortened to Pioneer Corps, as this was regarded as a more 'martial' title that would attract more men to the service.

But one fact did please us – the word in metal 'Queen's' was not removed from our tunic shoulder straps. It gradually became known that the reason for many of the Labour Companies retaining the various regimental shoulder badges – a great honour – harked back to an action in the front line concerning a Unit of Welsh miners. [This is a popular urban myth: some shoulder titles were issued with company numbers but later an LC title was issued.]

They were tunnelling under the German lines to plant high explosives. Suddenly the Germans came over the top and captured the trench where the entrance to the tunnel was situated. The miners were left in a shocking dilemma because at that time no arms had been carried by the Works Battalions. Also, the news over the grapevine was that the enemy were not very keen on taking prisoners, so the decision was made to carry out a sudden attack on the Germans.

This onslaught was completely successful. Probably the odds were actually on the side on the miners. One can imagine the enemy reaction to the ferocious attack with tools as weapons in the hands of these fierce miners.

There is no doubting that a mining company was involved in an unarmed action against a German trench raid but this had little consequence in the issuing of shoulder titles.

14

JULY 1918

Now the weather became ideal for us: everyone was able to keep clean – a godsend. But the long marches resumed along with musket practice and bayonet attacks on bags of straw representing the enemy.

I also became aware of the absence of our heavyweight boxer, Joe, and also the famous Private Sharp. The pugilist had received fourteen days' leave to England and had gone underground for the duration. Sharp had returned from England and had been already involved in two other escapades, culminating in him being transferred as a hospital orderly (good luck to the patients!).

15

AUGUST 1918

One Sunday, August 4 we were fortunate to receive a 'day's rest', the first part a four-mile trek for a drumhead religious service followed by another long trek to the butts for rifle practice. After our return we collected the midday meal and the brassy voice of the sergeant major was heard outside the tent, calling my name.

Naturally, I wasn't quick in answering, wondering what further chores were in store for me. Thus I received a sarcastic enquiry as to whether I was going deaf.

The outcome was the information that I was to proceed on leave next day, but first to the Quartermaster's stores to claim a soap issue and take ablutions in the nearest flooded trench.

Next morning there was a medical inspection followed by a journey to Calais, homeward bound after sixteen months away across the Channel. Arriving at the leave camp around tea time I found that the accommodation consisted of bell tents erected practically in the sand dunes.

Next morning (August 6) there was naturally an air of excitement as the prospect of boarding the leave boat drew near. Everyone was congregated on the parade ground. Orders rang out that all armed men were to step forward. Then the others were marched away to the embarkation quay whilst we, somewhat perplexed, were sent back to the tents.

As the day wore on we were mustered again and issued with five rounds of ammunition apiece. We were grouped in sections of about a hundred men, each under an officer. We were sent out to roam around the streets and thoroughfares of Calais.

Several hours elapsed and whatever we were expected to do was not accomplished and we were marched back to the camp and every man handed back the cartridges fully expecting we would be homeward bound on the morrow.

But a heavy air raid took place during the moonlit night and there was a direct hit on the engine room of the next leave boat. In consequence no one was able to travel to England that day.

We all just hung around whilst the camp staff tried out plenty of bull: it had little success against experienced campaigners like us. After partaking of the evening meal the armed parties were paraded once more. But the only weapons issued on this occasion were French clubs.

Each man received orders to insert his club up his tunic sleeve and once more commenced marching around the streets of Calais still not knowing what this was all about.

The actions may be in response to events at Val de Lièvre where there is evidence that the distribution of socialist literature may have influenced the nature of the protest. This mutiny of artisans and trade unionists enrolled in the Royal Army Ordnance Corps took place in the Val de Lièvre workshops, near Calais. At many of these camps dissatisfaction over food, hours and pay were motivating factors. Grievances were communicated through the Messing Committees but no action was taken. Some twelve months before the Armistice matters came to a head at Val de Lièvre in the form of a stay-in strike. There is a pamphlet by A. Killick ('The Story of the Calais Mutiny 1918', published by Spark, 1968). There had been a more serious uprising at the notorious base training camp at Étaples in 1917 when the troops became fed up with the tough regime there. There was also another rebellion in Calais in January 1919 over delayed demobilisation.

My party arrived back at the camp fairly late, becoming increasingly annoyed at the way events were shaping. No one knew what was required of them, who or what they were to apprehend.

So to the next day: we paraded again and were issued with the clubs up our sleeves. In command was a fresh officer. We set off for another round of trudging through the streets accompanied with plenty of ribald comments from our ranks, increasingly bolder as it was realised that the officer seemed somewhat scared.

Sometime later we were halted across a fairly wide thoroughfare lined with shops and many estaminets. Further down the street a mob loped along with loud shouts. The leader attacked a man standing in front of an estaminet, raining blows on the unlucky fellow. He was left unconscious on the pavement.

Then the cavalcade moved towards our party. As they neared it was apparent that each man was armed with a black revolver or a bayonet. They never hesitated confronting us – we were the hesitant ones.

The officer squealed out 'Don't let these men through' and then retreated to the back of the column, which just opened up like dockyard gates to allow these miscreants passage. Several of us had narrow escapes from the whirling side arms as the gang rushed down the street.

Then the officer regained his voice. 'You deliberately allowed those men to pass'. He took a book from his pocket and added, 'All names and numbers, please'.

He had written several of these when he received another jolt. A knowledgeable soldier confronted him with a poser. 'Were you in front leading the men when this rabble arrived?'

The officer did not reply and the soldier continued. 'In that case I will take your particulars also. An officer must lead his men at all times.' The result of this encounter was that no names or numbers were taken and tea and buns were provided and paid for in the YMCA – guess by whom.

An officer paid for tea and buns in a YMCA canteen in order to extricate himself from a possible charge of cowardice. Establishments where soldiers could buy food and drink ranged from substantial Expeditionary Force (EF) canteens to one-man enterprises in holes just behind the front lines. The first EF canteen was opened early in 1915. Later in the war regiments and battalions opened their own canteens. There were more modest canteens than the big army variety, run by organisations such as the Salvation Army, the Church Army and the YMCA and others. By 1918, indeed, there was an enormous array of canteens (mostly dry, some wet), buffets, clubs, brasseries, soup kitchens and coffee stalls. On the usual pay of a shilling a day the soldiers, especially married ones sending money home, really struggled to afford a daily egg and chips and 'van blong'. It was made even worse by a steady inflation of prices throughout the war. Regimental and battalion canteens tended to be cheaper than EF canteens but this came to a halt in 1918 when a 5 per cent discount given by the EF to them was discontinued (they had to buy from the EF). It was possible to buy a large range of goods in canteens, and most camps had several canteens to choose from. In the headlong retreats of 1918 some large EF establishments were captured by the Germans, but not before the fleeing Tommies had eaten, drunk or otherwise removed their stock.

The next day the band of deserters was arrested by a show of proper force – the garrison troops were ordered out and armed with machine guns and rifles. Trapped between two large forces of these heavily armed men the mutineers were forced to throw down their revolvers and bayonets (obtained from a Military Police post they had raided).

It transpired that the deserters were troops shipped from Mesopotamia and sent straight to France without leave. They had rebelled against this – hence their behaviour. There was a Court Martial carried out on the leaders and summary justice meted out to these ringleaders. Of course, I was delighted to arrive home again, a place I had not expected to see again, only an old double-fronted shop situated on the Isle of Dogs but heaven to me. It was quite obvious that the shortages of food and supplies were depressing everybody at home.

The one thing that greatly irritated me was the number of times I was asked when I was going back when I had been home only a day or two. Eventually, the day of return did arrive and I made my way through Calais once more. I had made up my mind (for obvious reasons) not to tarry in this place overlong.

I arrived back at Sylvestre Capel later that day, only to find that the Company had moved on. My only recourse was to travel on to the R.T.O. at the railhead to get directions.

On 8 August 1918, the 4th Army counterattacked at Amiens (well south of where George was working). The 10 Division attack was led by Australian and Canadian Divisions which had been kept in reserve during the many retreats. Later to be known as a 'black day for the German Army' (Erich Ludendorff), advances of up to 4 miles along a 15-mile gap were made in a single day and over 16,000 prisoners and 330 guns were captured. This attack was a prelude to the advances of the entire Allied Army. Labour Companies were now diverted from building defences to maintaining buildings and maintaining roads and railways over newly captured ground. At the end of the month 132 Company was transferred to Puchvillers, 8 miles north-east of Amiens (3rd Army) to work on road construction.

He told me they had moved south so I made tracks to follow them. I found that I would have to abandon the railway at a certain point and make my way by any possible means. I found myself on familiar ground on the road to Courcelette.

Nearing this, I had to pass a vast column of German prisoners. These men were in a desperate condition. Some had most of their clothing taken from their bodies by explosives. Most had been wounded. It appeared they had experienced a terrific bombardment.

These men could be described as the enemy but in actual fact they were no longer the enemy. All I had in the way of cigarettes etc. were doled out to them as I passed. It made me realise that hostilities were reaching their last phase.

I finally arrived at the place where the Unit was quartered for the time being. There was bad news: some casualties had occurred. A shell had burst amongst them on the road to Ytres. A Lance Corporal had lost his life and some half a dozen were wounded. This particular NCO had served in every campaign from the Afghanistan War onwards. He was aged over fifty. [It is nearly impossible to identify this man; he was not an original member of 132 Company, but he could be 76396 Corporal Joseph Samuel Heath.]

16

SEPTEMBER–OCTOBER 1918

It was now the second week in September. The new camp was situated in a very depressing area, an environment which resembled a vast graveyard – the scene of the Third Battle of Cambrai. In one spot there were twenty or so wrecked tanks. The local rats were enormous. We all wanted to press on away from this dreadful place.

Towards the end of September it was clear that the German forces had begun to gradually fall back on all of the sectors of the Western Front. The 168th [132] Labour Company experienced an extremely busy time: bridges and roads all had to be repaired, all kinds of transport and equipment had to be attended to.

All these tasks were carried on unceasingly till just after the first week in October when news arrived that probably the strongest and most impregnable line of defence in history had been captured by the Allies (October 9). Everyone realised that the war would be over in a matter of weeks.

This is the Battle of the Hindenberg Line when in nine days British, French and US forces crossed the Canal du Nord, broke through the Hindenburg Line and took 36,000 prisoners and 380 guns. German troops were short of food and had worn out clothes and boots, and the retreat back to the Hindenburg Line had terminally undermined their morale.

17

NOVEMBER–DECEMBER 1918

We moved into more zones of utter desolation. News of the Armistice came when we were in Salesches, north-west of Englefontaine. We celebrated throughout most of the night around a large bonfire, toasting the peace with whatever could be obtained in the way of stimulants. [The unit was to remain in the Englefontaine area in the Forest of Mormal until it was disbanded in March 1919.]

In a few days we were marching to our final billets in France before joining the armies of occupation on the Rhineland. Our new town was Englefontaine, situated on the outskirts of the Mormal Forest, which covered a very large area. As we entered the town during the dusk of the evening one could discern dozens of bodies littering the ground near the roadway and the surrounding forest glades.

In the official Report on Labour the following was noted – 'The last stages of the fighting found the V Corps confronted by the great obstacle the Forêt de Mormal (20 miles east of Cambrai). Only indifferent forest roads lay through this barrier; but owing to the great efforts put forward by 132, 153, 157 and 70 Labour Companies a splendid highway was made and maintained, enabling traffic and communication to be kept up without a hitch.'

December had now arrived and everyone seemed to be enjoying this new tranquil and safe place. The main body of the Company was kept busy repairing and patching the local roads. One small detachment was employed at a sawmill a mile or so into the forest.

The Sports Officer had become busy and again I was noted down as the goalkeeper in the soccer team. So instead of digging about on the roads the time was spent in exercising and running around the countryside. Baths were also available.

Within a few days matches were arranged with various Units. The team travelled sometimes as far as Valenciennes to compete in these games. Plenty of hospitality was received in the same spirit as the bruises were. I personally got my full share of the latter! Being a goalkeeper in those days one was never allowed to comb one's hair or rub the ball around the chest to clean it before punting it up the field. Wherever the ball was the boot followed it as a matter of course.

One morning, as a change from procedures, the Sports Officer suggested that instead of running exercises it would be a good idea to perform a little ground work on the football pitch. This was carried out forthwith: who's going to argue with an officer?

The team was busily engaged on this task when the sound of a military band was heard nearing the town. When we broke off from our labours for elevenses it was discovered that the Devonshire regiment had arrived.

This was extremely interesting: did they possess a football team? During the afternoon the Company runner (me) was sent on his cycle to ask this question.

Oh – what spit and polish! I even had to state my business before being allowed inside the gate and allowed to go to the Orderly Room. I was pointed out to the R.S.M. – whose name was Quantrill.

'Yes – we do have a football team', he replied in answer to my query. 'Be happy to give you lot a game in about a week's time. Suit you?'

I replied that the Sports Officer would have to confirm the date and left his presence. As I was about to leave I realised that there might be a canteen round about. I did find one but was informed of the absence of any beer. However, I wanted biscuits, chocolate and cigarettes. The conversation veered round to why I had visited the Devon's headquarters and I gave the information that our Unit wanted a friendly match with them.

This seemed to cause some amusement amongst those gathered there so I remarked that our team was very good – seven professionals and an amateur county player were amongst our eleven. They retorted that the Devon team consisted of eleven professionals and one (the captain) was an international. If I had any money left, they said, I should spend it at the canteen before leaving so I wouldn't be able to lose it on a bet on the result.

'Horsefeathers!' I remarked to myself as I cycled away. Whoever heard of a Regiment being able to commandeer eleven professionals and so complete a team in one go. It's not possible! I arrived back at the playing field and informed the Lieutenant that a match could be arranged but I didn't bother to tell him of the conversation in the Devon's canteen.

He was very pleased that a game was in the offing. He would take the cycle and travel down and confirm the date and time of the match. He did this later and arrived back with the news that the game would take place on the following Thursday at one thirty. Early lunch would present no problems as it was usually issued from the quartermaster's stores on the previous evening.

The Lieutenant thought it was a good idea for the recognised team to have three practice games on Saturday, Sunday and Monday against selected teams from the Unit, and follow this with running and other exercises during the remaining period.

To these sagacious observations everyone present nodded their heads vigorously. He went off on the cycle whilst it looked as though we would have to spend another couple of hours preparing the field. But suddenly our star player fell to the ground with muscular cramp. After a few minutes vigorous rubbing it was decided work would be called off for the day and that running would only take place during the following morning – the afternoon would be left free. Saturday would also be to ourselves, leaving the afternoon for the first practice game.

We were thus back in our billets around three o'clock and I found my pal Philip already sitting around a nice fire talking to our next door neighbour, a wonderful old native approaching eighty five years of age. He was the local wood carver and made most of the clogs, or sabots, worn round the neighbourhood.

I could understand very little of his conversation but Philip was picking up the language extremely well. It appeared that Monsieur had inherited local woods rights from the 'Lord of the Manor' and was thus never short of supplies – both for his work and for fuel.

I replied that we didn't own any of these rights but we were never short of wood for the fire, which caused a lot of laughter all round. The Frenchman's eyes were peculiar – they always seemed to be unblinking and ringed like a fowl's. So he received the nickname of 'Chicken Eyes', but not meant in any unkind way.

It appeared that on the arrival of the German occupying forces he just stayed put and was not molested in any way and really carried on a good trade with them in souvenirs and knick-knacks. He also tilled a small piece of ground for his vegetables, and a pot of stew or soup was always available on his small stove.

He was really a kindly old fellow who was wanting for nothing. After our laughing and joking around our fireplace I suddenly remembered my purchases that morning at the Devon's canteen. I handed the old fellow a packet of biscuits and some chocolates. Well – he almost salaamed me and knighted me on the shoulder, figuratively speaking! He had seen nothing like this since the outbreak of hostilities.

As a result of these friendly overtures after the football team had finished the two hours running stint the following morning Phil and I were invited into the old man's home to partake of soup and coffee. It was a very nice interlude for us two, away from home for so long a time. We were still sitting round the old chap's fireplace when the call went for evening cookhouse and we reluctantly had to leave the stew we had been served.

It looked as if this was made of small rabbit joints and I thought it wasteful to use such small animals. It wasn't till a week later that I discovered that we had been eating squirrel. I happened to be praising his cooking one day and, with the help of Philip, trying to get across how wasteful it was to use such small rabbit for the pot. But, by his actions showing animals bounding up trees I soon realised it was squirrel.

Philip nearly choked with mirth and exclaimed we had been eating squirrel stew. But that was the only meat the old man was able to trap for culinary purposes. Well – the outcome of this was that we were able to provide him with variety for a change. What a nice old character he was!

The time arrived on Saturday for the first practice session. Even in these small-time type of games the underdogs were out to show the ones who toiled not, nor spun not, where they got off, and set about it in no uncertain manner.

Thus the team experienced a tough time. The next day on Sunday (December 15) afternoon was equally fierce and I finished up as a casualty. The leg that had been injured at cricket practice was jumped on and badly bruised. I also received a cut on the knee so once again I was compelled to use the officer's stick and forget football for some time.

I decided to rest and have a quiet time on the Monday after receiving some medical attention. In the morning I just evaporated into Old Chicken Eyes' next door, sitting gazing into his fire and peeling roast chestnuts which only he seemed to know where to find in the forest.

Later that evening the Sports Officer called to enquire about my injured leg. I was able to convince him that there was no possibility of being able to take part in the game on the following Thursday. He left with the knowledge that a substitute goalkeeper had to be found.

Personally, I was not in the mood to worry about what happened. I seemed to be receiving more than my fair share of bangs and knocks in the sporting activities. I thought it would be a good idea to lie low and keep in the background with the aid of a liberal use of plaster on the leg, till after Christmas. Probably by then the Company would be entrained for the Rhineland.

The most restful place I was aware of was the abode of Old Chicken Eyes, the wood carver. The old fellow always welcomed me whenever I appeared. It was never boring watching him at work with timber and tools.

I managed to while away most of the time in this place till the day of the big match. I thought that I would hobble along to the sports field with the other spectators. The pitch looked good after all the work on it. Cars arrived with some notables from as far afield as Valenciennes and also the local (reputed) owner of the great forest, accompanied by his two nieces.

The contest that followed was extremely revealing: undoubtedly, the Queen's Company had to be very good, with seven of the eleven earning their living at football in civilian life. But, to my amazement, they suffered a twelve to two drubbing at the hands of the Devons. [It is interesting to note he still refers to the Queen's Company – by now they would have nothing to identify them as members of the Queen's Regiment.]

Not so much the 'hands' as heads because the Devons used theirs a lot, both to head the ball expertly and use their brains. It was amazing how, once the ball was obtained, the Devons kept it for long sessions. They simply passed the ball amongst themselves with uncanny accuracy, a lot of it by heading – a complete team of head jugglers.

In the centre of this onslaught, directing operations, was the redoubtable Sergeant Major Quantrill. I have often wondered but never verified whether he was the international player. If he wasn't he should have been.

As my unlucky deputy goalkeeper left the pitch, trying to regain his breath, he uttered the word 'Blimey!'

Christmas was now fast approaching and it was suggested that a concert might be arranged. A tentative date for it was Boxing Day. Philip was given permission to manage the arrangements. He asked whether I would be willing to help.

'Not as an actual turn,' I replied rather hastily, 'but in other capacities', and so it was agreed. The village (or church) hall was not large so it meant seats had to be limited, although there would be plenty of standing room.

One great need was for a piano. Where was one of these coming from? Chicken Eyes helped us out on this one: he said there were three of these instruments up at the Château and that it was likely we would receive the loan of one of them.

As soon as possible we called at the big house and were received in a very friendly fashion and granted the loan of a piano for the Christmas period. The preparations took place all through the week preceding the festivities and were completed on Christmas Eve.

Christmas Day was an entirely different affair to the one in 1917 when the Unit was bombed from the air at Brielen. The concert took place on Boxing Day as arranged and was a complete success. All the vocals were marvellous. Phil possessed an excellent tenor voice. The songs were the favourites of the early years of the nineteen hundreds, ballads like 'Thora', 'Asleep in the Deep', 'Blighty', 'The Miner's Dream of Home', 'Fall In and Follow Me', and, of course, all the ditties which were the rage of the time.

The place had to be tidied and put right afterwards and we had to return the piano to the Château. Philip had quite a long chat with the master of the house. He had been to the concert with his two young nieces and was informing my friend that he had enjoyed the evening. At the same time he invited the pair of us to dinner one evening. The invitation was accepted.

During this conversation I could only look and smile and nod: before the New Year we strolled along the drive to the Château and enjoyed the best meal since before the war.

18

JANUARY 1919

A little later preparations were in full swing for the inevitable trek to the Rhineland. I was lucky again to count myself amongst the baggage crews. A long march was in prospect for the main body of the Company to the railhead at Valenciennes, where we were to entrain.

132 Company did not join the Army of Occupation. They remained in Englefontaine and undertook prisoner of war escort duties. George will have transferred to another, unknown, company. Eleven labour companies moved into Germany excluding divisional companies etc. It is quite possible his whole section (twenty-eight men), were transferred together to make up numbers in a different Company.

I was caretaker of a large load of kitbags so was able to rest my still bruised leg. About an hour after the Company's arrival we were chugging along in an easterly direction. I was one of four men in a truck full of so many bits and pieces that there was hardly room left for us to occupy.

But we soon got to work and got it all ship-shape. It soon became apparent to everyone that a great deal of time was to be spent on this journey. The permanent way and track was in a shocking condition. Frequent stops were inescapable. When looking ahead of the train after the driver had halted one could observe gangs of workers, sometimes even replacing the rails.

At least twice a day when stopping, ration parties made up of German prisoners brought food to the trucks. It wasn't long before the tinned food began piling up in our truck: the contents of the sandbags were enough to feed twenty men – all this to take care of the needs of four men.

One fellow excelled himself with an extremely bright idea, as follows: the first German home near the border should receive the food surplus in the form of a coconut shy. I didn't think that this was sensible, to say the least, pointing out that one family could not take the blame for a whole Nation.

As further weight to my argument I remarked that in the act of throwing the tins there was a possibility of someone overbalancing and hurtling down the embankment.

Another couple of days elapsed before this senseless manoeuvre was accomplished. The train was travelling particularly slowly past what looked like a rail worker's abode. We had steamed past a place with a rather German-sounding name. He who had thought of this brilliant scheme pelted the building with the spare tins of rations, joined rather half-heartedly by the other two. Despite all the effort not a window was broken and after another five miles it was discovered that we were still travelling through Belgium. What a welcome bonanza for the occupants of that cottage!

Eventually, Cologne was reached and the Company got off the train and entered the city looking like the offshoot of a guards' brigade – extremely smart and efficient. For a change our headquarters were right in the heart of the city at the end of the Hohe Strasse (High Street).

These buildings were former German barracks and were extremely well-equipped: each man had a bed and locker. There were separate dining halls and the basement was furnished with shower baths and washing and drying machines – something I had never seen before.

Next day work allocations commenced: a party of eighty five including me were sent on a detachment to a district four miles north of Cologne known as Nippes. Here we were to labour under the direction of the Royal Ordnance Corps. The place was in no way appealing: it looked like a glorified junk yard occupying a very large area with rail connections to the main line.

The Detachment suggests he was now part of either 41 Company (ex 2nd Infantry Labour Company Lincolnshire Regiment) or 78 Company (ex 13th Labour Company King's Liverpool Regiment), who travelled from Forêt de Mormal on 5 January 1919.

Practically every instrument of war was on view in this establishment – at least two thousand guns, the great majority of which were damaged. I was fairly certain that an extremely long gun (the whole party could straddle along it) was originally known as 'Big Bertha'.

Another building about the size of Waterloo Station contained damaged aircraft of all types. The largest were wrecked Gotha bombers, the planes which had attacked the ill-fated Canadian troops opposite the St. Jean Clearing Station near Ypres.

The exterior body work of the fuselages of the Gothas looked perfectly normal, with the coating of dope. But on examining the interior body work one could see that every kind of cloth had been utilised to cover the frame-work. I could even detect blue material covered with white spots which looked like table cloths. They must have been desperately short of material (and their Allies) towards the end of hostilities.

The detachment were back at the main headquarters in a very short time because so many men were getting duffed up on their way back from the city at night. The only remedy was the harsh one of confining them to barracks. Finally, one unfortunate received a bullet in the foot, and, either by accident or design, the place ignited and we were sent back to the main body.

Now that the Unit was amongst thousands of troops once more the Sports Officer was around. 'You'll be alright now, Weeks, won't you?' he declared. 'I'll put you down for goal again, is that alright?'

'Yes, sir,' I replied. 'Three bags full, sir.' (actually, I only imagined the last four words). So I was down in his little book again. This time no friendlies were booked: the team was entered in the Rhine Army Cup. But looming over our shoulders was the news that the pesky Devons were now in the Army of Occupation. Who wanted to meet them again?

19

FEBRUARY 1919

There did not seem to be any immediate work for the returned detachment from Nippes. One morning I was asked to report to the Orderly Room. On my arrival I learned that being the only dock worker on the strength it was proposed that I become promoted to non-commissioned rank and take charge of the Ordnance Corps detachment which was commencing work at the Cologne docks despatching clothing and equipment to all parts of the occupied country.

I was completely taken by surprise – stunned for the time being, so the Orderly Officer said 'Go away and think it over and come in again later with your decision.' I left the Orderly Room with my mind in complete turmoil. I was totally bewildered.

My immediate pals saw that I was in a bit of a state when I entered the billet and I soon explained what had been conveyed to me. The older man said, 'George, you'll have to do the job if there is no one else. Life could be made hell for you, otherwise. So think it over very carefully.'

Allowing for a reasonable span of time to pass I reported to the Orderly Room, where I was asked if I had made up my mind. When I answered in the affirmative I was informed that I was to be promoted to Sergeant – right there and then, and, after another six weeks to Company Sergeant Major.

I replied that I would take charge of the operation at the docks but was not inclined to accept any promotion. This caused some disbelieving stares on the other side of the fence, but finally it was agreed that I would proceed that afternoon at 4 p.m. with the party.

The parade caused problems: included in the party of eighty men was a sergeant and lance corporal. Naturally I expected the Sergeant to order the men into formation in order to march away. But this he vetoed, saying that if I was in command of the party I was the person to take charge in every way.

So that obstacle was surmounted. It was a little difficult at first because, not being used to shouting commands, my voice was a mite shaky at the outset but it soon improved as we marched towards the docks, especially after numerous 'Eyes rights' and 'Eyes lefts' (Cologne was flooded with brass hats).

We arrived at the dockyard amidst a great deal of merriment and ribald comment – even the sergeant was wearing a broad grin. I reported to the officer in charge. He was very surprised I was in charge of the party but soon conveyed to me what was to take place.

Most of the work was confined to loading bales of assorted clothing into railway box cars from various upstairs floors and gantries by means of wall cranes and 'snotters'. The shifts for the job would be from four thirty till eleven p.m. [The supplies for the Rhine Army were shipped in along the Rhine from Rotterdam, hence the need for 'dockers'.]

When I got back to the men and informed them of the conditions and times of work they were delighted: most of them thought they would be required to work throughout the night. Now, it seemed that a good night's rest would be ensured, and that most of the day would be free for their normal pursuits, one of the most popular being visits to as many canteens, YMCA and Church Army and as many other establishments as possible in order to purchase cigarettes, chocolate, biscuits and other goodies.

You see – one of the largest black markets ever known had already started in the city and was now in robust health. One could hardly blame the ordinary soldier: Cologne was a desolate place to be without money – and what was the British soldier's pay? – peanuts!

For some weeks things travelled happily along: the men were getting very efficient and some jokingly asked if I would recommend them for a docker's card when they returned to England.

20

MARCH 1919

But the lance corporal got into a scrape by breaking safety regulations: he sallied through one of the warehouses puffing away on a huge briar pipe without a care in the world. But he was soon under lock and key. He had always maintained that his uncle was the famous Sir William who had risen from the ranks to place a baton in his haversack. However, the general consensus of opinion was it was only a case of their names being similar.

This will be Field Marshal Sir William (Willy) Robert Robertson, 1st Baronet, GCB, GCMG, GCVO, DSO (29 January 1860 – 12 February 1933) he was the first and the only British Army soldier to rise from private soldier to field marshal having joined as a trooper in the 16th Lancers and rising to become Chief of the Imperial General Staff in 1916.

Unfortunately, this pleasant project came to a rather untimely end (I would never had got a crown on my sleeve, anyway). There are always black sheep amongst the shorn lambs: a few greedy erks in the working party put an abrupt end to our operation. After around three weeks into the job just a few men were not satisfied in being able to go queuing in their leisure time through the day at the various canteens (most of their purchases were bringing in around five hundred per cent profits).

No – they had to start pilfering Army stocks at the docks. Some erks even did not bother cleaning their underclothing and socks in the ample machines provided for this but simply opened the bales, extracted the new garments and, quietly went up through the roof traps to change, disposing of their soiled articles over the back of a huge gravity tank.

Eventually, these discarded garments were piled high above the tank (or even flung carelessly inside it). Another racket was to take pairs of service boots out every evening. These were disappearing over the wall at around one hundred marks a pair.

Matters came to a head one night: I had the men paraded and was about to give orders to move off when a top brass appeared on the scene with several flunkies. I could detect in the gloom a terrific amount of movement in the ranks.

I discovered later that the contraband was being rushed rearwards towards a boundary wall. It came out later that a friendly sentry did a lot of clearing up after we left the precincts of the docks.

Next day (Wednesday, March 19), needless to say, was the end of the work in the docks and I was left wondering what the next project was going to be. I was not left guessing very long: shortly I was making my way to the headquarters of the Rhine Army Embarkation Staff situated on the banks of the river.

This party consisted of a sergeant, corporal and six privates, all fully armed. We now carried the American Winchester rifle. The Enfields had long ago been exchanged for these.

Arriving at the Embarkation Office the sergeant entered for instructions and soon came back with the news that we were to board the former Rhine river pleasure cruiser named the *Kronprinz Cecilie* as a guard.

The information afforded us was that this vessel went to Rotterdam from Cologne and back once a week. It conveyed troops, stores and, in fact, all the needs of a modern Army. So the project before us seemed exciting as we climbed aboard the fine-looking paddle steamer lined up alongside the wharf.

We were shown to our new quarters, which were excellent – very nice, comfortable bunks. Everything was good and clean. We were paraded in front of the new C.O. He spoke in a fairly friendly manner, stating that he wasn't keen on people stamping around at all hours with rifles at the ready. None of us argued with that!

'One thing I have to inform you of, men,' he barked. 'I want everybody looking busy at all times. It matters not if at that moment nothing is being done.'

We called this 'acting'. We were then dismissed for the rest of the day and decided that the best thing to do was to keep out of sight for the time being.

Next morning we plucked up the courage to mount the stairs (companion way) and made our way up on the deck. We noticed that the officer was in the wheelhouse alongside the actual captain of the ship, a German civilian. We thought it would suit us if he actually stayed in the bridge house.

The sergeant appeared and requested that we parade with all our arms and ammunition. He told us that on entry to Holland all these articles would be locked away and secured till Germany was reached again. This operation was then carried out. All the weapons were placed in a large locker, locked securely and the key taken to the officer. It seemed to be a funny way to guard a ship!

The journey to the Dutch port took nearly two days. It was quite pleasant and relaxed – just needed to remember to move around when one saw the officer approaching. One thing was apparent to us all – the officer seemed intent on learning the rudiments of navigation. Perhaps he was thinking of taking up a seafaring career once he had left the service?

On reaching Rotterdam we were struck by the quaint appearance of the dock area: even windmills were close at hand. We discovered that whatever cargo had to be discharged or taken on board was to be moved by us – the guard. This was no great shock – it was something for us to do and we got on with it without any fuss.

Some military goods were already piled on the quayside. Having discharged our cargo we soon got this on deck apart from some artillery wheels. These had to be rolled down the gangplank. What seemed a good suggestion at the time was to form a man chain and pass the wheels to each other.

I happened to be in the position nearest the ship and owing to the steep slope leading up to the quay the first wheel gathered so much momentum that there was little chance of controlling it. I just escaped being struck by it. It hit the vessel's hull with an almighty bump before disappearing into the murky waters of the dock.

There followed an ominous quiet: all eyes were glued on the ship to see if anyone was about. They would surely investigate such a heavy bump. But, to our relief, nobody appeared so it was apparent that the ship was deserted. Yet the problem facing us now, apart from the price of an artillery wheel (some-one placed a figure as high as twenty five pounds on it) was to make sure the loss remained undetected.

So the remaining wheels were loaded quickly and a rapid search was rewarded with an old canvas sheet to cover up the articles. We fervently hoped that no one would notice the missing wheel in Cologne.

The first member of the ship's staff to arrive back from town was the sergeant, who was pleased that we had covered up the wheels – obviously, to protect them from the weather. He didn't know that we six miscreants had another 'cover up' in mind.

The first halt on the voyage back was at a small town called Duisberg, where the vessel was moored for the night. Some of the civilian crew went ashore for amusement and relaxation: but the following morning there was evidence that a disturbance had occurred – such as cuts and bruises. We got into conversation with one man who had received a nasty swollen eye. He stated that his party had been set on by 'Reds'. They may have been Red Indians for all our knowledge of who the 'Reds' were. It made my mind up that I would give this town a wide berth on any future visit.

We were surprised that when the ship entered German territory no move was made to get out the rifles. We concluded that our C.O. knew what he was about. This mission suited us – who wanted to lug rifles around? Not the six musketeers!

As the vessel approached the marvellous city of Cologne we were in conference about when it suited us to discharge the cargo – preferably when the officer and sergeant were away from the ship. So it happened that way – everything was passed ashore without any fuss, the old sheet draped over the wheels to prevent any quick counts. When we were summarily dismissed from the ship some two months later (for another reason – see later) the artillery wheels were still on the quay where we had stowed them.

The following day we were once more chugging along on our way and at our destination a similar operation took place as on the first trip – apart from an artillery wheel in the dock! The 'guard' stood by to handle cargo while the remainder of the ship's personnel went into town. We six put on our thinking caps and came to the conclusion that it was going to be rather dull visiting Rotterdam and only viewing it from the dockside.

So it was arranged that a couple at a time should visit the town. On their return another couple would do likewise. The first pair arrived back with the news they had visited a small café in the main thoroughfare. The female proprietor had given them an enthusiastic welcome when she recognised that they were members of the British Army.

It appeared that this lady's sister and her family had been saved from extreme danger in Ypres by British Tommies. Her gratitude was overwhelming and all six of us were invited to her café whenever we wanted to go. The two who had been there had been lavishly refreshed.

Well, it was concluded that our six healthy appetites would be too much of a drain even on a much larger establishment than this little eating house so the arrangement was made that a different couple would make the trip into town on each separate voyage.

21

APRIL 1919

E aster was now near when the news came that the vessel would miss a trip or two for maintenance to be carried out on the boiler and engine rooms. This left us free for a few days. So on Good Friday (April 18) I decided to visit headquarters to see some of the old and familiar faces. But, unfortunately, but fortunately for them, a large number of them were excused duties for the day. Some of them had gone on a voyage on a river cruiser to Koblenz through the region of the Seven Mountains.

The Sports Officer appeared and was very surprised to see me. He asked after my injured leg. In fact, I had forgotten that I had suffered an injury.

'Good, 'he said. 'I'll put your name down for the team. There is a match tomorrow afternoon.'

I had no answer to this: I was committed. So the following afternoon I was standing between the sticks, keeping in a cup semi-final. I forget what competition it was but I do know that our team lost two-nil and that I finished up with a finger in a splint and a determination that I was not going to be persuaded into any more football games while I remained in the Army.

But he returned to goal in civvy street and suffered even more broken this and broken that while playing for various Isle of Dogs amateur teams, mainly in more mud – on Hackney Marshes. He was well into his thirties when he retired and then suffered more agonies supporting Millwall FC.

After the short break for repairs there was another trip to Rotterdam. On arrival I was still wearing the splint so was not required to work on the cargo, making me an automatic choice for a trip into town. I called at the café mentioned previously.

A really nice welcome was given to my companion and I. Various foods were brought to us to choose from but as the meat and fish selection seemed to be a bit on the raw side I felt safer with egg and chips. Later I learnt that the consumption of viands in a practically raw condition was a Dutch national custom.

In Cologne the various rackets were progressing merrily along. There were magnificent products obtainable in the city for chicken feed – beautiful razors and cutlery from Solignum, all kinds of musical instruments etc. A handsome profit was easily available when these various articles reached across the border.

22

MAY 1919

We made fifteen trips, always stopping at Duisberg on the way back. We were looking forward eagerly to the bright lights of the town on one trip but all day I had been trying to throw off an impending attack of migraine. Sufferers from this disturbing malady need darkness not brightness so I stayed in my bunk despite the cajoling and wheedling to come and enjoy myself from my mess mates.

Finally, they went off ashore. Some time later I was visited by the sergeant wanting to know in what direction the 'ginks' had gone. I could only say they went ashore. He pointed out it was nearly ten-thirty and there were [sic] no sign of them coming back. He told me to wait another ten minutes or so and then proceed ashore to look for them.

This request or order pleased me not one little bit. 'Sergeant,' I replied, 'I have a terrible headache and I've never even set foot on the banks of this town. I wouldn't know which direction to take.'

'Well,' said the sergeant, 'no help for it, you'll have to go. The skipper's ashore somewhere and as I am in command at the moment I have to stay aboard so wrap yourself up and go and look for them.'

But just I started to put on some extra clothing a crescendo of shouts and cries came from the quayside so I shot up the companion way and made towards the gangway to meet them.

Not only were they arriving but also a crowd following in their wake. It was soon very clear that the pursuers only wanted one thing – blood! The five came hurtling down the gangway, their aim to reach the safety and security afforded by the ship.

They were followed by a hail of missiles: one of them, a wine or spirits bottle, shattered above my head and a piece of glass hit my left ear. This was the last straw! I hadn't been anywhere – just resting quietly in my bunk and now I had a gash on the ear.

I was going to make sure I didn't suffer any further damage so I quietly made my way back to our quarters and put some plaster on the ear. The row outside had subsided. The excursion party entered: all had suffered minor damages. It appears that there had been a disagreement with the infamous 'Reds', whoever they were. We had heard a lot about them.

I told them there would be some further disagreements in the morning. Who with, they wanted to know? 'The sergeant,' I said. 'He was not pleased.'

The upshot of it all did not bode well for our future on this nice job. Perhaps the others knew the game was up – there was not a great demand for the usual excellent breakfasts, just mugs of tea. We moved off, the engines generating the power needed against the volume of water descending from the distant Alps.

We were all well aware that as soon as the vessel berthed in Cologne we would be proceeding in the direction of the Hohe Strasse and our headquarters. It was not long before the sergeant made his presence felt, informing us that he was personally delivering us back to 'Old Bull and Brass', as he put it. We had to tidy and spruce up the quarters ready for a new outfit, who, he added, would not get such an easy and pleasant time as we had been enjoying.

Proper guard duties would be introduced and the rifles would be got out frequently – more work for him, he complained. When he had finished his dirge we were nearly heartbroken for him.

We proceeded with the allotted tasks as the spire of the Dom drew nearer. Someone remembered that the rifles had been inside the locker for a very long period. What was the condition of these weapons going to be?

Our fears were justified: to clean these weapons it looked as if more than one session was needed so everyone had to buckle down with a will. Who ever heard of a dirty rifle in Cologne?

During the 'discussions' with the sergeant all six of us had been classified as wrongdoers by him. So, to me, he seemed determined to return all six of us to base. But I decided that there wouldn't be any protestations of innocence from me. I still had something up my sleeve to use as self-protection: I still had the splint on my long finger.

At base we were met by the sergeant major in an extremely terse manner. He managed to book us an interview with the Orderly Room for that same evening. We were awarded seven days confined to barracks.

Following this we were introduced to the kitchen and cooking staff: some hours of enforced labour were in prospect, such as washing up crockery and preparing vegetables. I collected a large bowl of crockery and dropped the lot on the floor, caused by my injured finger. The sergeant cook was more than a little annoyed and upbraided me for my clumsiness. I indicated my finger and pointed out that if the bowl had contained the china from the officers' mess that would have been really disastrous.

At this point one of my five comrades from the river boat chipped in with the information that I had been awarded fatigues wrongly, explaining the circumstances to the sergeant, who seemed to listen with sympathy. The outcome of this on the following morning was a plum job.

I was directed to a large mobile water tank fitted to a cart with orders that after breakfast each morning I was to connect a hose to a tap and fill up the tank and then I was free for the remainder of the day. Things could not have been resolved better if I had planned it all.

23

JUNE–AUGUST 1919

By now the army was demobilising at a fast rate. The Army of Occupation was also being cut back in manpower but the stores were maintained in place if there was a need to reinforce. Most of the Labour Units in Cologne were given a new task of maintaining stores and horses in Germany for the troops should they return.

I knew that another home leave was pending but it was just as bad being home without cash in the pocket as here in Cologne. Now six hours a day was available for canteen queuing and trading in the purchases!

This was a universal industry in the A.O.O. (Army of Occupation). You could also pick up manufactured goods which were almost given away. Great quantities of this stuff were being sent home by the occupying forces. This was eventually prohibited by High Command because of the adverse effect of the volume of these articles on the transport and communications system.

I managed to secure the water job for six weeks, then was practically compelled to go on leave. I wasn't too keen as I was having such a glorious time in the Rhineland. I found circumstances at home extremely black, to say the least. Thus I pondered over the decision I had made earlier in the year when I had turned down the offer of promotion. My own profession in the docks was in a precarious position. Men were even trampled, flattened and badly injured in the fights for work at the dock gate calls.

I was now a little way past my twenty first birthday, in extremely good physical shape. My weight was around thirteen stones, vastly different to the nine stones odd I scaled when I joined up.

I came to the conclusion, given that I would be demobilised before the year's end, that my future in civilian life would be to join the Society of Stevedores, a union where membership was practically hereditary from father to son.

At first my father adamantly refused to sponsor my application. Then I reminded him what had happened to the scholarship application papers I had taken home for his approval and signature during my school days. He had simply tossed this document on to the kitchen fire.

After long arguments I achieved my objective and when I travelled back to the Rhineland I was a member of the Stevedores Society – very little aware of the toil, sweat and numerous injuries which awaited me in the docks.

24

SEPTEMBER – NOVEMBER 1919

O n my arrival back at the Hohe Strasse I was amazed at the ease I garnered the cushy water job back. But the snag here was that other little tasks had been added to it. There were now several Women's Auxiliary Corps Units based around the district, all requiring male assistance in the rough kitchen work, such as fuel, water, garbage dispersal [sic] etc.

It was not so much the actual work but the bull and discipline which were rife in these women's bases. Every WAC with stripes and upwards laid down the law to me. My one and only consolation was that this treatment would only have to be endured for a month or two.

The major setback here was that no longer could I command the time needed for the lucrative shopping sprees. I had to resign myself to the fact that there was not going to be a great deal of collateral when finally I would be demobilised.

I did enjoy a couple of Sundays (September 28 and October 5): instead of turning up for religious service I went to Bonn to join a river cruise to Koblenz and back. The church services were a real pain, especially from upper crust WACs who gave me such a run around. In contrast the cruises were quite enjoyable, with refreshments provided and music from a military band.

The weeks passed by and old members of the Queen's were being demobilised in increasing numbers. On November 3 my turn to go arrived. I travelled down the Rhine to Rotterdam on the very vessel I had been employed on for quite a time earlier in the year.

The next day I survived an extremely rough passage across the North Sea to Harwich. I got to Crystal Palace where I spent the night and was granted demobilisation leave the next morning – November 5, along with the princely sum of nineteen pounds in my pocket.

George worked, usually in Millwall Docks, for the next forty-four years as a stevedore, a physically exhausting job, often in similar conditions to those endured on the Western Front, and on arduous materials such as cement, flour, dangerous chemicals etc. He had several serious injuries, including a broken neck in his fifties.

But there were some good times, especially in the 1920s, when a good-looking young man (see the photograph on page 84) cleaned up after work and travelled in fashionable clothes to various West End theatres. He was always in work, always in a successful gang of stevedores, which often secured plum jobs, such as the import/export of motor cars – a lot cleaner than cement and much better paid.

George settled down in 1929, marrying a local girl, Ivy Hill. They had a daughter (Irene) and a son (Alan). As a married man he developed his passion for motor bikes, especially very large American ones, such as a Henderson and an Indian 4. He was able to service and repair all his prized bikes.

The family did very well out of this: on many occasions we enjoyed camping weekends in Kent after roaring down on one of Dad's motor bike combinations on Saturday afternoons after he had finished work. Not many families on the Isle of Dogs enjoyed the sun, beaches and orchards of Kent as often as we did.

He was also extremely skilled with fabrics and wood – he could repair any piece of furniture (remember how he was so enthralled with Old Chicken Eyes).

My Dad died in his sleep at the age of 84 in 1982.

APPENDIX: WAR DIARY OF 132 COMPANY LABOUR CORPS

Once the Labour Corps formed in April 1919 units were instructed not to keep war diaries. This diary has been researched over many years by trawling through GHQ, army and corps diaries looking for references to 132 Company Labour Corps. Some of the original entries are contradictory and there are large gaps (particularly in early 1918). Grid locations are as listed in the diaries at the time.

17 Mar 17	24 Coy Queen's (132 Coy) arrives BOULOGNE for employment in FIENVILLERS-CANDAS with 5th Army
18 Mar 17	Moves to ATHEUX to relieve fighting troops working for RCE (V)
13 Apr 17	Company detachment of 2 officers and 223 ORs moves from MAILLY-MAILLET to CANDAS for road construction
13 Apr 17	As a result of Army Order 611 the Labour Corps is formed. 24 Infantry Labour Company the Queen's Regiment is to become 132 Labour Company. All personnel are renumbered between 78,601 and 79,200
16 Apr 17	The detachment moves from MAILLY-MAILLET to Roberts Huts AVELUY – Dumps and railway crossing
12 May 17	Groups formed (a group co-ordinated the activities of a number of companies within an area – these formed before the Labour

Corps officially formed and for a short while some maintained a war diary):

54 Group – 2 (Permanent Base) and 132 Companies and 65 and 73 PW Companies

13 May 17	½ Company now at No 2 Aircraft Depot temporarily detached to 1st Army
30 May 17	Back Area – 5th Army
	54 Group – AVELUY – 132 Coy and 2 PB Coy and 65 and 73 PW Companies
1 Jul 17	Company HQ still on River ANCRE (57D/W.11.d.cent) with a detachment (2 officers + 194 ORs) at CANDAS with RFC and a detachment of 125 men as rail guards
9 Jul 17	10 ORs joined from UK 30 ORs evacuated to UK as unfit
11 Jul 17	Moves to RE camp at AVELUY Chateau
23 Jul 17	30 ORs detached to 4th Army School of mines at RIBEMONT
26 Jul 17	Detachment at CANDAS (1 + 141) moves to MONTIÈRES
27 Jul 17	Company HQ moves to TOUTENCOURT (3rd Army, 52 Group) for forestry work with 27 Canadian Forestry Corps
4 Aug 17	Detachment of 1 officer and 50 ORs sent to work in Quarry at MONTIÈRES until 15 Aug 17
9 Oct 17	Company and 41 Company moves to POPERINGHE and re-joins at 5th Army (XVIII Corps, 43 Group) to work on Light Railway maintenance and construction and road work
15 Oct 17	XVIII Corps
	31 Group – 27/L.6.a.8.8. – 17, 49, 65, 132, 141, 148 and 192 Companies
16 Oct 17	All units: 17, 45, 65, 132, 141, 148 and 192 Companies now under command 31 Group. All working on Lt rail except 132 and 148 Companies who are allocated to corps tasks
23 Oct 17	1 man wounded
28 Oct 17	Remains in situ but now supporting II Corps. Located at B.26.c.6.1.
13 Nov 17	Group under orders to move to VEZELISE (Nr NANCY). Following Companies involved: Det 79, 132, Det 137, Det 200, Det 735 and 740 Coys and 8, 66 and 121 PW Coys and 52 Coy Chinese Labour Corps and 25 Indian Coy

There is no further record of the unit until the German offensive in 1918. George Weeks' diary suggests they remain in the Ypres area working on roads and light railways.

8 Mar 18   Units: – 5th Army AQ Diary

Northern Sector

57 Gp – BARLY – 4, 6, 47, 48, 132, 188, 723 and 728 Coys and 168 Coy CLC

26 Mar 18   22, 43, 132 and 136 Companies transferred to IX Corps (2nd Army) to act as GHQ Reserve 2nd Army AQ Diary

10 Apr 18   Distribution of Labour on building GHQ Defence Line:

'C' Sector

57 Group – Sub-Sector C3 – BARLY

  6, 47, 48, 65, 138 and 728 Companies

  And 168 Coy Chinese Labour Company

    Sub-Sector C4 – 4, 132, 188 and 723 Companies

17 Apr 18   Number of men in white companies capable of bearing arms: 55 Officers, 12 WOs and 1641 ORs, from the following Companies 3, 4, 6, 31, 35, 43, 84, 92, 94, 110, 131, 132, 136, 138, 151, 174 and 728 Companies

18 Apr 18   6, 132 and 138 Companies change of command from 5th Army to 2nd Army (VIII Corps).
132 Company moves from HAUTEVILLE to BLARINGHEM (27/N.35.b.2.5 – 26 Group) still on GHQ Defence Line

29 Apr 18   Labour Commandant GHQ Defence Line – ST-OMER
26 Group – located EBBLINGHEM (27/T.12.b.1.4.)
6, 132 and 138 Companies – GRAVECOURT FARM (27(SW)/N.35.b.6.3.)

9 May 18   Move to WINNEZEELE 27/P.36.a.8.2 (31 Group, VII Corps) from 27/N.35.b.2.5 still on defence work

10 Jun 18   Instructions from GHQ reference the arming of companies. Up to 400 rifles per coy and 150 rounds of Small Arms Ammunition per man. The following sector of the defence Line are to be manned as follows:

WESTHAZBROUCK Sector (VII Corps)

5 Group – 12, 13, 55, 61, 94, 111, 132, 164 and 178 Companies

9 Jul 18   5 Group – 12, 13, 61, 94, 111, 132 and 164 Companies transfer in situ to XV Corps. Still working on trench construction

	WINNEZEELE Defence Line
	132 Coy located South East SCHOONEN BORST (27/V.5.a.7.8)
13 Jul 18	Reorganisation
	5 Group – 6, 13, 20, 48, 61, 91, 111, 129, 132 and 824 Companies and A Coy 1 Battalion Cape Coloured
31 Jul 18	Moves to WEKE MEULIN (27/V.15.a.5.5)
18 Aug 18	12, 13 and 132 Companies transferred from East to West HAZEBROUCK Line working for Commander Royal Engineers 40 Division
29 Aug 18	13, 132, 138 and 164 Coys – sos to 3rd Army – XV Corps Diary
29 Aug 18	132 and 138 Companies move from 2nd Army to PUCHVILLERS 57D/R.29. (V Corps – 3rd Army) on road construction for Commander Royal Engineers
2 Sep 18	Moves 57D/R.29. to 57C/M.25.b.4.8 for road work
16 Sep 18	Moves 57C/M.25.d.4.8 to EPEHY 57C/O.35.b.8.2 for road work
5 Oct 18	Moves 57C/O.32.b.8.2 to 57C/Q.35.d.2.3 for road work
9 Oct 18	Moves 57C/Q.35.d.2.3 to 57B/S.14.b.2.8 for road work
14 Oct 18	Moves 57B/S.14.b.2.8 to 57B/O.12.a.1.2 for road work
19 Oct 18	Moves 57B/O.12.a.1.2 to 57B/O.6.b.6.7 for road work
7 Nov 18	Moves 57B/O.6.b.6.7 to 51/S.20.d.5.0 for road work
Nov/Dec 18	The last stages of the fighting found the V Corps confronted by the great obstacle the Forêt de Mormal. Only indifferent forest roads lay through this barrier; but owing to the great efforts put forward by 132, 153, 157 and 70 Labour Companies a splendid highway was made and maintained, enabling traffic and communication to be kept up without a hitch – Report on Labour in BEF Appendix BB
28 Nov 18	Joins 37 Group (V Corps) which consists of 32, 113, 119, 120, 128, 132, 142, 148, 153, 157, 161 and 700 Company, 280 and 287 Area Companies
8 Dec 18	XIII Corps (70 Group) takes over command located ENGLEFONTAINE S.20.d.5.0.
20 Jan 19	7, 72, 79, 132, 167 and 169 Companies transferred, in situ, to Line of Communication from 3rd Army in order to provide PW escorts.
14 Feb 19	7, 72, 79, 132, 167 and 169 Companies due disbandment
6 Mar 19	67, 79 and 132 Companies disbanded

Casualties

According to the Commonwealth War Graves Commission the following are listed as having died in 132 Company. The figures are remarkably low considering that throughout the period October 1917 to March 1918 they were in the Ypres Salient. When they moved south after the German offensive they were mainly employed building defences and were not subject to any of the German attacks.

BARWICK, Private, C.G., G/46305. 24th Labour Coy. The Queen's (Royal West Surrey Regiment) transf. to (78652) 132nd Coy. Labour Corps. 22 December 1917. VI. BB. 29. Mendinghem Military Cemetery – Poperinge, West-Vlaanderen

LAKER, Private, F.E., G/55742. 24th Labour Company. The Queen's (Royal West Surrey Regiment) transferred to (Cpl. 78615) 132nd Company, Labour Corps. Died of nephritis 6 December 1917. Age 32. Son of John and Sarah Laker; husband of Annie E. Laker, of 18 Cleveland Park Crescent, Walthamstow, London. Native of Walthamstow. XXXI. B. 22. Étaples Military Cemetery, Pas de Calais.

MARKS, Driver, H., 3198. 3rd Battery, 4th Brigade, Royal Field Artillery transferred to (633999) 132nd Company, Labour Corps. 26 November 1918. Age 25. Son of Mr J.S. Marks, of West Down Farm, Littleham, Exmouth, Devon. II. B. 15. Caudry British Cemetery, Nord.

PERKINS, Private, Arthur, 78954. 132nd Company, Labour Corps. 16 January 1918. Age 35. Husband of Ruth Elizabeth Perkins, of 54 Clarendon Road, Hoe Street, Walthamstow, London. Panel 160 and 162A and 163A Tyne Cot Memorial, Zonnebeke, West-Vlaanderen.

STEVENS, Private, George, 1369. Depot, Royal Fusiliers transferred to (326611) 132nd Company, Labour Corps. 22 September 1918. Husband of Mrs G. Stevens, of 1 Salisbury Street, Burdett Road, Bow, London. C. 31. Five Points Cemetery, Léchelle, Pas-de-Calais.

TAYLOR, Private, G.E., 49119. Labour Company, The Queen's (Royal West Surrey Regiment) transferred to (79034) 132nd Company, Labour Corps. 16 January 1918. V. C. 46. Bard Cottage Cemetery, Leper, West-Vlaanderen.

WADE, Private, C.T., G/49125. 24th Battalion, The Queen's (Royal West Surrey Regiment) transferred to (79053) 132nd Company, Labour Corps. Drowned 16 January 1918. Age 37. Husband of Jessie Elizabeth Wade, of 77 Milton Road, Stoke Newington, London. V. C. 47. Bard Cottage Cemetery, Leper, West-Vlaanderen.

Honours and Awards

Every man would have received the War Medal and Victory Medal, and those serving before December 1915 will have received a Star. All these medals were issued reflecting the original unit (Queen's Regiment). Any man conscripted direct into the Labour Corps, i.e. after April 1917, would have had Labour Corps engraved in the rim of the medal.

There are only two recorded awards to the Company. The following were awarded the Meritorious Service Medal (MSM): 78605 Sergeant Stephen Gowers and 78632 Lance Corporal Harold S. Grout.

INDEX

If you enjoyed this book, you may also be interested in…

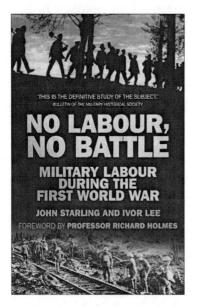

No Labour, No Battle: Military Labour during the First World War

JOHN STARLING AND IVOR LEE

978 0 7509 5666 6

From 1917 British soldiers who were unfit or too old for front-line service were to serve unarmed and within the range of German guns for weeks or even months at a time undertaking labouring tasks. Both at the time and since they have arguably not been given the recognition they deserve for this difficult and dangerous work. From non-existence in 1914, by November 1918 Military Labour had developed into an organised and efficient 350,000-strong Labour Corps, supported by Dominion and foreign labour of more than a million men. Following the war, the grim and solemn tasks of clearing battlefields and constructing cemeteries, which continued until 1921, were also the responsibility of the Corps. Here, John Starling and Ivor Lee bring together extensive research from both primary and secondary sources to reveal how the vital, yet largely unreported, role played by these brave soldiers was crucial to achieving victory in 1918.